Follow Me

Becoming a Lifestyle Prayerwalker

Randy Sprinkle

new
hope
PUBLISHERS

Birmingham, Alabama

New Hope® Publishers
P.O. Box 12065
Birmingham, AL 35202-2065
www.newhopepublishers.com

Library of Congress Cataloging-in-Publication Data
Sprinkle, Randy, 1949-
Follow me : becoming a lifestyle prayerwalker / Randy Sprinkle.
p. cm.
Originally published: Follow me : lessons for becoming a prayerwalker, c2001.
ISBN 1-56309-948-9 (pbk.)
1.   Walking-Religious aspects-Christianity. 2. Intercessory prayer-Biblical teaching. 3.
Bible-Textbooks. I. Title.
BV215.S67 2005
248'.5--dc22
2005010863

ISBN: 1-56309-948-9
N054120 • 0606 • 2M3

To the Intercessors

Known to God because they were a gift from Him.

Given, they then gave of themselves for years
to see this book come to your hand.

I am humbled by their love and sacrifice
and I am irredeemably in their debt.

Table of Contents

Foreword

By Steve Hawthorne
Author of *Prayerwalking: Praying On-Site With Insight*

Prayerwalking is so simple that the only teaching you need is that which would keep it from getting complicated. The trouble is, we are already complicated. That's why we need a book like this. I see three ways that we are complicated regarding prayer. Each is dealt with by what you'll find as you walk through this book.

The first complication in prayer that I see today is that we usually prefer a mediator. We seem to think we'll do better if someone else gets through to God for us. Of course, God loves people to intercede for each other, but it's not hard to get lazy and let someone do your praying for you. It makes as much sense as having someone eat for you. Although the Bible is clear that there is "one mediator" (count 'em: one! 1 Timothy 2:5), we like the convenience or comfort of having an expert, higher-tier prayer person to broker our urgent requests.

Second, we usually prefer to learn a procedure of prayer that is guaranteed to work. We seem to like having prayer as an option for emergency problem solving instead of as a way of life, like breathing. Kind of like having a hammer to break the glass in case of fire.

Our third complication is doing prayer as a program. Programmatic religious life is structured so that spiritual matters are relegated to certain areas, times, and buildings. The missions conference comes once a year. The prayer meeting is on Wednesday night. And so on. Our lives have been splintered for so long that we can't imagine what a 24 and 7 life in God might look like. To some, it sounds like going to church all the time. To walk with God all day every day might actually be what we were made for. It could be the life you always wanted.

Get ready for adventure, because Randy Sprinkle's book guides you step by step—literally—along a pathway where you get next to God and join Him in filling the earth with His glory.

Regarding the first complication of wanting a mediator, there is a relational immediacy in the very idea of walking with God. No expertise is needed because it has to do with how powerful and close God is, rather than with how clever or advanced you may be.

You are as qualified as you are close to God. Here's something amazing: this book rests on the remarkable assumption that God really wants to condescend to walk with people like you and me. Go ahead. Be astounded. It wouldn't have to be that way. You may need to turn your expectations inside out: This book will not certify you as a higher-level intercessor. It's really all about God coming down to street level. In Psalm 18 terms, it's not so much about God training your "hands for battle" (verse 34) so that you become a prayer expert; it's really all about how "Your [God's] condescension makes me great" (verse 35).

Regarding a second complication, our penchant for procedure, you might be disappointed if you want recipes or guarantees. No cheap techniques to make God move quickly here. No formulas for counter-spelling particular evils. Instead, get ready for a life-long walk with God. You're going to learn some sure-footed wisdom to pray with persistence with increasing hope. You'll learn to pray with Scripture and pray toward God's purpose instead of praying about your problems.

Regarding our habit of relegating prayer to program, you're going to pray outside the lines of conventional "request management" prayer. If you walk, as the title suggests, with Christ so as to follow Him, you are going to pray beyond the bounded, dated, boxed, and listed prayer affairs. You're going to pray in ways that surpass the confines of the predictable, scheduled part of your life that you may have called your "prayer life." Walk very far following Jesus as this book suggests, and you won't be able to sort out the prayer part of your life at all. You may lose interest in praying before you do things. You may find that prayer becomes the way you do anything.

Take the title and subtitle seriously. This is not about doing prayer stunts to amaze your friends and fill church pews. It's a very personal invitation from Christ Himself. He's not asking you to copy Him, imitating Him in a few ethical decisions. He's calling you to come with Him as companion and accomplice in fulfilling His mission. As you follow Christ, you'll find that it's really not about praying outside. It's about praying onward toward the culmination of God's purpose in all the world.

Within a day or so of beginning to make your way through this book, you will find yourself praying beyond the walls of your home. You'll be praying beyond church services and buildings. You'll pray yourself past boundaries you didn't know existed. Because you are aligning your life with Christ with every step, you might find joy in the idea of praying beyond the borders of your country, blessing people in distant lands. As you pray with God's heart, your prayers will begin to lock in on the completion of God's purpose: that Christ be known and followed by many from every people group on earth. Your life will be simplified, because it will be centralized on what matters most—on Christ and His glory.

—Steve Hawthorne
Austin, Texas

Introduction: A New Day

"Are you doing anything Friday night?" our neighbors asked.

The question was almost ludicrous. What seminary student has money to go out on a Friday night? It was the spring of 1975 and my wife and I were studying in Fort Worth, Texas, preparing for missionary service in Africa.

"No, we're not doing anything."

"Well then, would you like to go to a prayer meeting with us?"

By God's own sovereign workings, prayer had already become a passion in our lives as well as a joyous opportunity of fellowship with the Savior we loved. A Friday night prayer meeting actually sounded far more appealing to us than dinner out or a movie. When the appointed time came we walked down the street to our neighbors' and rode with them to a simple frame house. Inside we met four or five others. The discussion quickly turned to the reason for our gathering.

The downtown Main Street area of Fort Worth during the mid-'70s was a concentrated area of bars, strip joints, porno parlors, adult book stores, and peep shows, as well as a center of prostitution and drug trade. Responding to a God-given burden for the people of the area, as well as those who were being drawn in from the whole Dallas-Fort Worth metroplex, these few men and women had begun to seek others who might have a similar burden. The area was a place of darkness and bondage and the people who frequented it were in need of the liberating light of Christ. Over the next few weeks, prayer and discussion resulted in a ministry plan. None of us had any prior experience in or leading to street ministry, and the makeup of the group was evenly divided between those of us planning to be missionaries and those who were preparing for the pastorate. Yet God was clearly leading us out into the streets of this city. We felt completely inadequate for the task but we were willing. Knowing that we didn't have a clue as to how to begin, we had actually begun correctly. What was to become a fruitful ministry had begun the way every ministry of Christ's church should begin: disciples on their knees seeking His plan and power out of hearts willing and eager to follow Him.

An Unexpected Delay

Quickly a pattern emerged. Each Friday the team fasted in fervent prayer as we went about our seminary and job schedules. At 6:30 p.m. the team met for corporate prayer in preparation to hit the streets. By 8:00 or 8:30 p.m. we were downtown, walking and talking with men and women in the party atmosphere of the night, sharing the truth about God's liberating love with them, inviting and exhorting them to receive Christ as the new Lord of their lives. The first months of the work were both exciting and frustrating. We knew the truth. We shared it logically and passionately. We won a lot of arguments—but we weren't winning any people to the Lord. In addition to this heartache, another problem was emerging.

In the early weeks we were constantly in conversation with what seemed to be a steady stream of people. Slowly, though, we recognized that we were becoming known by the "regulars" and they weren't interested in talking with us anymore. Where we had been talking for hours at a time with people about God's love and provision for them, we were now walking for hours with few conversations about the Savior. Suggestions to use the extra time for more prayer brought us face-to-face with a dilemma. We believed that focused, reverent prayer required bowed heads and closed eyes. How could we pray and keep walking the streets at the same time? Compromising God's glory was not an option. Carefully, without really realizing it at the time, we began to develop a practical theology of in-the-world prayer.

Why did we bow our heads when we prayed? We were expressing reverence for God's glory and awesome greatness. How could we stop doing this? God showed us that bowing our heads in prayer was indeed pleasing to Him, but actually it was just an outward reflection of an inner attitude. He was more concerned with and pleased by our hearts that were bowed down in reverent humility and dependency. That understood, we could now consider raising our heads as we walked and prayed on the streets.

But what could we do about the issue of closing our eyes as we prayed? Everyone agreed that we did this out of learned habit, but it had a practical basis as well: it enabled us to shut out the world so we could focus more fully on the Lord (and we were certainly walking and ministering in a place that had worldly temptations and distractions). How could we ever focus on prayer in a place like this if we opened our eyes? His answer was one of singular challenge and double meaning.

"Try it and see."

We did and immediately we were seeing as we'd never seen before.

A New Way

Walking among and talking with people had been our method of engaging a lost world with the saving gospel. We were still walking and talking, but now it was with God on behalf of this same lost world. And that made all the difference. Our preparatory prayer, both personal and then corporately as a team, had been and remained essential. But this walking prayer brought a new level of encounter with God as our hearts were moved in more intense and directly personal intercession for the people we saw and encountered. We were moved. God was moved. And very soon we discovered that the people on Main Street were moved. But how could open-eyed praying be more focused when it seemed the distractions must make it less so?

In the early '90s a former missionary told me of his return to the states to pastor a large downtown church. Though he was undeniably called of God to this new ministry, the first year's experience was not what he had expected. Instead of growing into the role, he soon found himself exhausted and despairing. At just this time Dr. Bill Bright, founder of Campus Crusade for Christ, came to speak at the church in fulfillment of a long-standing invitation. Later at Sunday dinner the conversation found its way to the pastor's impossible situation and the question, "Dr. Bright, how do you thrive with a load that I know is far larger than mine?"

Dr. Bright's response was God's word of breakthrough into a new day and a new way of ministry. "Have you ever heard of the Holy Spirit?"

Years earlier on the streets of Fort Worth, we, too, found our answer in the ministry of the Holy Spirit. When we moved out into the world with clean, prepared hearts, eager and willing to be the Church in the world, we found that the world had lost its power to distract and inhibit. The Spirit of Christ could now lead us and we would respond. Unhindered in us, He enabled us to see like we'd never seen before and to pray like we'd never prayed before. The tangible evidences of this new "praying on-site with insight" as Steve

Hawthorne, author of the book *Prayerwalking*, calls it, was not long in coming. Even in a simple greeting or the innocent query, "How are you?" we recognized a difference in people. There was a softening; the thick skin of resistance toward God was suddenly thinned. There was openness. We could see it. We were able to speak a word of love, extend a genuine touch of care.

The prayer that moved near the people of the world was being used of God to move them nearer to Him; soon people dead in sin were being born into new life. Even though we had not yet heard the term, we were prayerwalking. And just as Jesus taught the disciples, we were seeing the kingdom come.

Some History of This New Way

Any time a new movement arises and gains participants, historians begin to study its origins. A blessed characteristic of the modern prayerwalking phenomenon is the absence of all the basic historical elements. There is no early catalytic leader. There is no identifiable birthplace or birthday. Even the one who coined the term prayerwalking is lost to history. What we do know is that the timeline seems to begin in the mid-1970s, and in standing at that point of observation we see the essentials of what we need to know about the origins of this modern-day activity called prayerwalking.

In the mid-'70s intercessors, scattered in various parts of the world, began to be called out of the church and even out of their prayer closets and into the world. This early activity was without either human initiation or organization, and occurred simultaneously and without an awareness of other prayerwalkers. Clearly, the Initiator of all prayer was the Author of this new initiative in prayer. It had divine purpose at its center, and in its birthing moment, kingdom timing. From the streets of Far East cities to the sidewalks of Fort Worth, Texas, Jesus was taking to the streets—and taking back the streets—and men and women were hearing and heeding His call, "Follow Me."

About This Study

You may be unsure how you have come to this beginning point. You may not have even known what prayerwalking was as you committed to begin this study. Of this, though, you can be sure. You are here by divine appointment and you are part of a sovereign work of God in this day. Your primary purpose over these next few weeks will not be to learn *about* prayerwalking but to *become* a prayerwalker. This book which you hold in your hands is designed to enhance that process. Its stories are true prayerwalking testimonies.

The structure of this study is simple and the lessons brief. Each week has five studies which are to be done individually. Only one lesson should be done in any given day. The studies themselves will take about a half an hour of time to complete, but the integration of the truths and correlated practices into your life will be an ongoing activity throughout the study and beyond. You are encouraged to move through this study in community. Meet weekly with a small group of like-hearted believers to discuss what God has said and done through your prayer and study. A facilitator's guide is included at the back of this book. If you do not already have a facilitator, choose someone to fill this enabling role or consider taking turns leading each week.

Intercession is prayer for others and prayerwalking is in-the-world intercession. In our self-guided and self-centered culture, the inclusion of concern and care for others is incongruent. In a God-guided and God-centered life, though, love for others is pervasive. As you move through this study you will recognize the changing of your life's orientation. Prayerwalking is not one more activity to try and fit into your already too-full life. Instead it has as a fruit the emptying and lightening of the life. You will find more time, less pressure, and greater peace and love as you follow Christ in this prayerwalk. May your hearts and spirits be eager and obedient, and may His kingdom come in your life in ever richer, deeper ways and in all the earth—even quickly. Amen.

Basics

Our study is designed to be utilized by individuals who study each day, practice what they learn, and then gather weekly with a small group to dialogue, clarify and expand understandings, and prayerwalk together. Each day's study is structured in three parts:

Beginnings
Throughout Today
Evening Reflections

Beginnings should be completed first thing each morning, Monday through Friday. This is to optimize integration of what you have learned by applying it as you go through your work day and to ready all the group members for a weekly meeting sometime during the weekend. If work or class schedules require, this element can be adjusted. The point is to complete the "Beginnings" study at the start of your day, whenever that is.

Throughout Today—These are thoughts or directions for use as you move through your day with the specific intent of allowing God to integrate the truths that you have learned into your everyday life. Personal discipline is required for this to be the beneficial activity that it can be. Take your book with you and pause for moments in the day and refresh what you are to do with God that day. He will do the rest.

Evening Reflections—In general, reflection is foreign to us as a people. It shouldn't be. Reflection simply means "to think back on" or "to consider." You may successfully do this in one of two ways: 1) Take ten minutes in the evening to think back over your day and your prayerwalking experiences and jot them down. Or 2) During the day, note in the provided lines observations or experiences as they occur.

In week 3, you will notice the addition of a fourth daily element: **Today's Prayerwalk.** Each day you will be encouraged, as part of that day's study, to engage in a brief personal prayerwalk. As you do this, you will be building on the truths that you have learned while being used of God to extend His kingdom of love into the world.

This entire study is structured to fit well with your morning quiet time of prayer. If this essential discipline is a struggle for you at this point in your life, it will help you begin. Remember, we are to discipline ourselves for the purpose of growing in Christlikeness. If getting up thirty minutes earlier each day seems impossible, here is a simple solution. Go to bed thirty minutes earlier. God often wakes us up but it is our responsibility to get up. Ask His help. Then as He gives it, discipline yourself to do it.

At the end of these few weeks you will be amazed at the difference in your life as you heed Jesus' words, "Follow Me."

First Week

Walking with God

"And what does the LORD require of you but to do justice, to love kindness, and to walk humbly with your God?" (Micah 6:8)

This week we will:
- learn God's original purpose for us
- understand how God's purpose is realized
- learn basic journeying principles
- meet our guide
- learn the way

Beginnings

Bow in prayer, thanking God for the journey you are embarking on. Invite Him to lead you into all the discoveries He has for you.

❧

Vance Havner once said, "Moving all the while and getting nowhere is not confined to rockers; plenty of people live that way." Our world says to us that fulfillment is found in advancing and acquiring. This is our purpose according to society. And the means to achieve it? Constant activity. God's Word presents a very different picture.

Open your Bible and read Psalm 46:10. What is the first thing God says we should do? _____

We should cease striving, take our hands off, and be still in His presence. In this place, in this way, we can begin to know Him and His purpose for us.

In the first chapters of Genesis, we read the account of God's creative acts: light and land, living creatures both small and great, plants of seeming endless variety. And in the midst of it all He placed the pinnacle of cre-

In the beginning, we were created to walk with God!

ation, mankind. Created by God in His image, we have characteristics distinct from other living creatures. The greatest of these is that we are created with a spirit. Since God is Spirit, this spirit element of our makeup makes possible the greatest privilege of all human existence: actual fellowship with the awesome, infinite God of the universe.

Let's look at two men in the Bible. Read Genesis 5:19–22 and 6:7–9. Who are the two named here?_____
What do these two men hold in common? _____

Enoch and Noah walked with God. Although we may think the Old Testament often describes people as "walking with God," it is quite rare. When we study this descriptive phrase, we find that it means the closest, most intimate and confidential relationship that is possible between the divine and the human.

Looking into the Garden of Eden, Genesis 3, we see life in all the perfection that God originally intended, with every provision, including the ultimate: regular, unhindered fellowship with God.

Read Genesis 3:8. Who came walking in the garden? _____
Who was seeking whom? _____
For what purpose? _____

In the beginning, we were created to walk with God!

Throughout Today

As you walk forward through today's responsibilities and activities, do two things:

1. Consciously think about this incredible truth:
I was created to walk with God.

2. Intentionally and repeatedly thank God for this wonderful privilege and praise Him for the joy and love we find in His presence.

Evening Reflection

What was today like in light of the realization that you were created to walk with God?

How did it feel to repeatedly thank God for His wonderful love for us?

Was it hard to discipline yourself to focus on Him and praise Him? If so, why do you think it was?

Week 1 Day 1

Beginnings

Bow in prayer and invite God this morning to show you His love.

❧

Into the perfect environment in which Adam and Eve lived and walked with God came "the serpent of old who is called the devil and Satan," the one "who deceives the whole world" (Revelation 12:9). These first humans were drawn into a dialogue with the devil that soon resulted in death. The perfect world, which was theirs to enjoy, became off-limits. Worse, the perfect walk, which had been their highest privilege and deepest joy, was now no longer possible. They had chosen to reject the truth and believe a lie, and in so doing had brought separation between them and the glorious God of light and life. They were now "dead in...trespasses and sin" (Ephesians 2:1).

But God, who is love and had created them in love, was not finished.

> ## *As we see the power of God's love for us, we glimpse just how much He loves fellowship with us.*

Man had brought a terrible dilemma: the pure holiness of God's character prohibited His co-mingling with the great object of His love, now tainted with sin. But God so loved them that He was willing to pay a terrible price that they might return to Him and their original purpose.

Read Romans 5:6. In our helpless state, what was the terrible price God paid to redeem us? _____

Despite our countless excuses, denials, and systems of so-called justifying acts and rectifying works, the truth remains—we are helpless to provide a worthy sacrifice for our sin. There was only one way. Someone who was pure and sinless had to make the sacrifice for us. Jesus Christ was the one. And He is now the Way back to God.

In paying this terrible, wrenching price for us, what was God showing? Read Romans 5:8._____

As we see the magnitude and power of His love for us, we get a glimpse of just how much He loves fellowship with us. He is willing to pay any price to make perfect fellowship again a reality—even the highest and most terrible price, the giving of His own beloved Son.

Sin prevented our living out the high purpose for which we were created by God in the beginning. It brought a great separation between God and us, a great canyon of separation over which there was no bridge. God made a way. Jesus is the Bridge. He is the Way back to God and the walking out of our original purpose.

Throughout Today

Before you start your day's duties, bow and thank God for loving you so much that He paid your debt. Think about this kind of love. How great it is!

Walk into the day thanking Him repeatedly and truly for His love throughout your day. (Note the special invitation on the next page. It is not part of today's study, but it is imperative that you complete it before you begin tomorrow's material.)

Evening Reflection

Have you ever had someone forgive a debt before? What did it feel like?

What was it like today as you thought about the debt Jesus paid for you?

How successful were you in repeatedly thanking God for His great sacrifice for you? Was it hard?

Was today the first day that you consciously and personally received Him as your Savior?

If so, what did you feel and experience?

Special Invitation

Before you can go any farther in this study and any farther in a desire to walk with God and labor with Him in the world, there is a question that you must answer. And you are the only one on earth who can answer it.

When film director James Cameron stood on the stage at the Academy Awards holding the Best Picture Oscar for his film *Titanic,* he declared that he was the king of the world. He borrowed his declaration from the young lead character in his movie and based it upon box office numbers that seemed to indicate that his film was the number one, most-watched film in all of history.

Not even close.

Just as the ship Titanic slowed to a stop and then sank out of sight, so did Cameron's film. The real number one film continued gathering speed and pulling away from the ever-more-distant runner-up. By the end of the twentieth century, the all-time most viewed movie had been translated into more than five hundred languages and seen by more than two billion people!

The real number one?

The *Jesus* film.

Cameron's story of the Titanic also missed what was perhaps the greatest human story of the tragedy. Fortunately it was not lost to history. And the story is greatest because of its tie to the greatest story ever told.

On board the Titanic was a widowed Scottish minister named John Harper and his six-year-old daughter. When the ship began to sink, Harper, traveling second class, handed his daughter to an officer on an upper deck who put her in a lifeboat. He then began helping those on his deck. Others were doing this as well, but Harper's assistance was unique because of his instructions, heard over and over during the chaos.

"Women and children and the unsaved into the lifeboats first. Women and children and the unsaved into the lifeboats first."

John Harper recognized the moment as the threshold of eternity. He was ready to face God, but he knew that many on board were not.

As a minister, Harper's lips had often declared God's love for the lost. Now his life declared it in an ultimate act. When he came upon a man without a life jacket, John Harper took off his own and put it on the man.

Later, floating in the emptiness of the dark chilling waters, a survivor came within sight of a man struggling to stay afloat. It was John Harper. Rather than asking for help, Harper called out to the man, "Are you saved?"

"No," came the answer.

"Believe on the Lord Jesus Christ and thou shalt be saved."

The man's reply was one of silence and they drifted out of sight of one another. A little later, the man spied Harper again and again Harper called out to him.

"Are you saved now?"

Again the answer, "No, I can't honestly say that I am."

And again the refrain, weaker but still clear, "Believe on the Lord Jesus Christ and thou shalt be saved." Then there was silence as John Harper slipped below the surface—and into the arms of God.

Later in a meeting in Ontario, Canada, the survivor stood, telling this story and closing with these words: "Shortly after he went down; and there, alone in the night, with two miles of water under me, I believed."

Long ago a prison warden in a place called Philippi came to his own "threshold of eternity" moment and asked one of his prisoners, a man named Paul, "What must I do to be saved?" Harper had been quoting that very prisoner's response.

Before you can go any farther in this study and in your life, you must answer one question that only you can answer. Are you saved from the just and due penalty of your sin?

If in your mind, the first thought is something like, "Well, of course. I'm a member of the church," or "I've been baptized," or "My parents were Christians and I've always been one, too," then you know what you are trusting in for your salvation.

Only in personally receiving Jesus Christ as Savior are we saved from the penalty of our sin and born again into new life. If you've never done that, today is the day. Don't wait another moment. Right now, receive Jesus. Then find a local minister or trusted Christian friend and ask for guidance as you are beginning your exciting journey with the Lord.

If you have received Christ as your Savior and Lord, this is a moment of joyous praise. Thank Him. Worship Him. Love Him. Walk into your day in a new grateful realization of the greatness of His salvation.

Week 1 Day 2

Beginnings

Bow in God's presence and thank Him for your salvation.

❧

In the glorious light of new life in Christ, we begin a journey that has no end, only ever-continuing steps of nearness and likeness to Him. The dilemma is that we still live in the same fallen world and that we live out this new life in the same old body. How then can we live as the new creations in Christ that we now are? We only know the old pattern, which is clearly not our way anymore. The model that continues to be set before us countless times each day is that of the world's ways. It is now easy to see that that is not the way either. How then are we to walk?

Read 1 John 2:6. What does God's Word say? _____
_____
_____

Prayer is not incessant talking to God but unceasing walking with God.

The answer is so simple and so clear. We are to walk out the Christian life as Jesus did. Immediately, the next question is, "How did He live?" With this question we begin the discovery of three essential elements in walking and living as Jesus did.

Read Colossians 3:16. What does this Scripture exhort us to do? _____
_____
_____
_____

We learn how Jesus lived by looking at His life; we may look at His life by looking in His Word. As we begin to see how He lived and how we should live, we soon make a startling discovery. It's hard! In fact, we don't seem to be able to do it.

At this point we face a critical choice: will we just settle for acting Christian or will we press forward that we might ever more fully and truly be Christian? In God's eyes the imitation Christian life is an unpleasing life. Read 2 Corinthians 5:7. How are we to walk? _____

_____

Read Hebrews 11:6. What pleases God? _____

_____

In the New Testament, faith is a key word denoting the foundational relationship into which we are called as believers. It is trusting God in everything. It is an attitude of the heart and an act of the will. Regardless of how things look, we look to God and trust Him. Jesus was able to walk an earthly life pleasing to God because He walked it in utter trust and expectant confidence in God.

Jesus was able to walk this way because He walked out His life in God's presence. Jesus was a man of prayer. Prayer, contrary to popular opinion, is not primarily asking God for things, but rather being with God.

Read 1 Thessalonians 5:17. How often should we pray? _____

We learned that God's original purpose for us was to have perfect unbroken fellowship with Him. Because we have been redeemed back to that original place and purpose, we can now walk continually with Him. Prayer is not incessant talking to God but unceasing walking with God.

Throughout Today

As you start into today's work, think about the truth of the Scriptures you have studied this morning. Thank God for the encouragement and strengthening they give to you as you walk into the day. Decide to live today depending on and trusting God.

Evening Reflection

Was it hard to trust God at any point today?

How did He encourage or guide you from His Word today?

What did you feel good about today?

Was it God-honoring?

Week 1 Day 3

Beginnings

Bow before God and invite Him to have His way in you today.

❧

When the disciples protested Jesus' announced departure from them, He took the occasion to reassure them with a wonderful new revelation: help was on its way.

Read Jesus' words in John 16:7. What descriptive name did He give this One who was being sent to them? _____

After this One's coming, would life be better or worse? _____

Jesus' words to their troubled hearts made clear that despite perceptions to the contrary, it actually was to their advantage that He return to the Father. Then the Holy Spirit would be sent to them, and in coming, He would be their Counselor, their Helper, their Comforter and so much more. But to live as Christ lived in this world of lies and deception, we must know the true way. Gloriously, the Spirit of God is also the Spirit of truth, and as such He guides us into truth. (John 16:13)

Is the Holy Spirit with us or in us? (John 14:17) _____

By this indwelling ministry we are transformed from acting to being Christian.

Not only has God brought the Spirit alongside us to guide and help us, He also has placed the Spirit in us. It is by this indwelling ministry that we are transformed from *acting* to *being* Christian. As we spend time each day reading in God's Word, we learn how Jesus lived and thus how we are to live. God's expectation, though, is not that we will go out and try with all our might to live this way. He knows we can't. When we try, we also learn that we can't. Instead the Holy Spirit takes the truth and our willing responsiveness and transforms us. We actually become more and more like Jesus. We are enabled to live like He lived because we are becoming like Him.

In his book *Mere Christianity*, C. S. Lewis said, "He is beginning to turn you into the same kind of thing as Himself. He is beginning, so to speak, to 'inject' His kind of life and thought, His *Zoe* [life], into you; beginning to turn the tin soldier into a live man."

Whenever we feel that we can't live as we should, remember Bill Bright's reorienting reminder to the overwhelmed pastor, "Have you ever heard of the Holy Spirit?" and look to our Helper-Guide in faith.

C. S. Lewis went on to say concerning the essential place of responsiveness as opposed to resistance in this tin-soldier-to-live-man process: "The part of you that does not like it is the part that is still tin."

Throughout Today

Rejoice in the reality that Jesus has given us the Holy Spirit to live in us and with us. We are not alone. We are not powerless. Rejoice! And as you do today, couple that praise with eager commitment to cooperate with the Spirit in every way.

Evening Reflection

What was it like today praising God for the power of His Spirit that now lives within us?

How did the Holy Spirit guide today?

Did He show you anything?

How did you respond?

Did you resist Him at any point?

Why?

Week 1: Day 5

Beginnings

Bow in prayer and ask God to reveal to you what it means to abide in Christ

❦

By looking at other's beginnings and endings, we gain valuable insight into how to live the time between the two—the time that is called life. In an upstairs room near the end of His earthly ministry, surrounded by a circle of confused and apprehensive followers, Jesus spoke some words that linked back to His first words to the disciples three years earlier. Together, these words formed the key to living the Christian life.

A metaphor is a phrase that, while not directly related to a subject, carries a resemblance to that subject and thus enhances understanding of it. When we sing "A Mighty Fortress Is Our God," the metaphor of a mighty fortress helps us understand an aspect of God's character.

Read John 15:5. What metaphor did Jesus use for Himself? _____

_____

_____

For us? _____

Probably most of us have pruned bushes or trees in our yards. After snipping off a limb, we may pick it up and hold it in our hand. It looks alive and identical to other branches on the bush, but regardless of appearance, we know there is a difference. It is dead. Why? Because it has no life in itself and it is now no longer connected to the source of its life.

What did Jesus say we, as branches, must do? _____

What did He say will be the result? ___

_____

_____

Foundational to the abundant life that

This searching world is not interested in imitations, and neither is God.

is intended for us as Christians is insuring that throughout each day, we as branches remain a part of the Vine—Jesus, our life. Apart from Him—out there on our own—we can only *act* Christian. We do not have the power within us to *be* Christian. Christ is that power. Our first responsibility is to ensure that nothing inhibits the flow of His life in us.

We may try hard, but we cannot exhibit the fruit of His indwelling Spirit: love, joy, peace, patience, kindness, goodness, faithfulness, gentleness, and self-control. We can only imitate it. This searching world is not interested in imitations, and neither is God.

Read Matthew 4:18–19. What was the first thing Jesus said to these first disciples? _____

_____

This invitation to the first disciples was the same invitation Jesus issues to us and to believers throughout history. These words are foundational to the Christian life. As we read in and think about God's Word, as we bow before Him—worshiping, listening, speaking—and as we then believe what He says and act upon it, we are following Jesus. We are living as He lived. We are following Him, and in so doing we are ensuring that we remain vitally connected to Him and His life-giving life. When we first answered His call to follow Him, we were grafted in as branches to the vine. In following we began to abide, and now in abiding we are empowered to continue following.

We are back to the purpose for which we were created in the beginning. We are again walking with God.

Throughout Today

Is there anything that Jesus has been trying to lead you into that you have resisted? Is there anything that is inhibiting His free, full flow into and through you? Turn from it and return to Him.

If you sense resistance in you at any point of obedience, this is the "tin" part to which C. S. Lewis referred. Resist resistance and immediately begin to follow Him. At that very point today, you will begin to experience Jesus' life in you and the fruit of His Spirit.

Evening Reflection

Did the Lord show you anything that you have been attempting to do on your own for Him? If so, what?

What did His Spirit reveal to you today?

Any points of resistance?

Any unconfessed sin?

What points of joy did you experience today as you walked with Him?

Second Week

Following Jesus
as
Prayerwalkers

KEY SCRIPTURE

"I am the light of the world. Whoever follows me will never walk in darkness, but will have the light of life." (John 8:12 NIV)

This week we will:

- explore Christ's kingdom command
- see how His kingdom comes on earth
- discover three types of intercessory prayerwalking
- understand the vitality of a prepared life
- begin learning the practical elements of prayerwalking

Beginnings

Bow in the presence of your risen Savior and praise Him for purchasing life for you. Ask Him to teach you to follow Him.

❧

The first and last recorded words that Jesus spoke to Peter were the same: "Follow me" (Mark 1:17, John 21:22). It is no different for us as disciples of Jesus. From our youngest days to our last, the great Lover of our souls is beckoning us to enjoy all the fullness of His life by becoming and remaining His followers. This seems straightforward until we discover an inherent paradox: central to Jesus' teaching about life are the words "lose it" (Matthew 16:24–25). Dietrich Bonhoeffer, martyred by the Nazis, said so truly, "When Christ calls a man, he bids him come and die."

Read John 12:24. What must happen to each grain of wheat in order for it to become a great harvest? _____

Every farmer knows two truths: 1) present in every grain of wheat is the potential to produce fifty or a hundred new grains of wheat, and 2) for this to happen the life of the single grain must come to an end. Obviously Jesus was not talking about our actual, physical dying. What did He mean?

Turn to Luke 9:23. What is necessary before we can follow Him? _____
Our lives before heeding Jesus' call were self-centered. In daily taking up our cross (our identification with Him) we both reiterate and reinforce our death to this old self-orientation. Our life is characterized by joyous, invigorating self-denial, rather than by the deadening self-indulgence of the past. Now not only *can* we follow Jesus, but we

> *As we follow Him, His purpose for coming to earth becomes our purpose for living on earth.*

will. Prayer, an unceasing, God-pleasing walk with Him, is the primary means by which we follow our Master. This life of following Jesus is a prayerwalk, and as we follow Him, His purpose for coming to earth becomes our purpose for living on earth.

Read Luke 19:10 and John 10:10. Why did Jesus come? _____

Jesus was sent to earth to seek the lost, save them, and bring them back to the walk they were created for, a walk of abundance and life with God.

Read Matthew 28:19–20. As Jesus left earth to return to heaven, what was His mandate to us, His followers? _____

Jesus promised His followers that He would make them "fishers of men" (Mark 1:17). The purpose for this was so that they (and we) might launch out onto all the waters of the world and bring the inhabitants to Him. We are not on mission to bring all the peoples of the earth to saving faith in Jesus, the Savior. God is. We don't have the power to do this. Only He does. We are simply invited, exhorted, commanded, and expected to become "laborers together with God" to this end. The earth will be filled with His glory and all the tribes and tongues and peoples and nations will come to worship Him as we faithfully do—as we follow Him.

Throughout Today

Consciously ask God to enable you to walk with Him today. As you work, be attentive to His purposes and cooperate with Him. Respond to His whispered words of love and direction with your own silent expressions of love for Him and immediate adjustment to His guidance and instruction. Be alert to opportunities to speak a word of testimony to someone.

Evening Reflection

How did you recognize God enabling you to walk with Him today?

Did you see Him accomplishing any of His purposes through you today?

What was the experience of God's love like to you?

At what points today did you adjust how you think or live?

Did you have opportunity to share a testimony today? Did you seize it?

Beginnings

Bow in prayer with the fresh conviction to die to your own designs. Confess to Christ your desire to live today in harmony with His designs.

❦

Marilyn vos Savant, who according to the Guinness Book of World Records has the highest IQ in the world, answers peoples' questions in a weekly *Parade* magazine column. The depth and breadth of her knowledge are such that if we found ourselves in conversation with her, no doubt our questions would seem endless. On the other hand, the One who has all understanding and wisdom, Jesus, had twelve men who traveled with Him night and day for three years, and as far as we know they only asked His instruction on one topic: "Lord, teach us to pray."

Regardless of their sketchy understanding on other important points, the disciples had grasped the fact that prayer was vital and that they were deficient in it. Jesus' answer, often known as the Lord's Prayer, has been carefully studied by believers of all generations.

The pinnacle of this cooperation is prayer— our desire synchronized with His desire.

Turn to Luke 11:1–4. In the prayer's priority of focus, who comes first, God or us? _____

As Jesus taught the disciples to pray, He taught them the supremacy of God and His kingdom in life. "Hallowed be Thy name." (May it be honored as holy.) "Thy kingdom come." The kingdom of God is of course not an earthly kingdom. It is rather the extent or range of God's rule. It began not with Jesus' coming but has existed and will exist throughout eternity. The only place that it is not currently present in full completeness is on earth among men and women.

We were created to rule over the earth. In other words, God, as sovereign Ruler over all, gave us the ability and authority to determine outcome by the application of choice. Sadly, we choose to reject Him and His rule. When John announced at the coming of Jesus, "Repent, for the kingdom of heaven is at hand," God was declaring that His eternal kingdom had come alongside and was now accessible to us. Person by person, as we turn from our own kingdoms (those areas of life where we have effective control) and return to His, His kingdom of love is extended more fully on earth.

Read Matthew 6:10. In this earlier and fuller teaching of the Lord's Prayer, what was the coming of His kingdom linked with? _____

How should His will be done here on earth? _____

We were made to live in harmonious relationship with God, to walk with Him. As we become part of His kingdom, we willingly place the things we control under His authority. We begin to experience the blessings and benefits of His life and care.

Our desires are reshaped by His desires and our decisions become more and more pleasing to Him. Through us, His will is being done on earth. We are learning that we are made not to operate independently as the world encourages, but as cooperators with God. The pinnacle of this cooperation is prayer—our desire synchronized with His desire. We live out those desires in faith in this conflicted world.

Throughout Today

Give thanks that God has come near us in love and drawn us into His kingdom of love. Be sensitive to those habitual exertions of our own will that are in conflict with His, and turn from them to His.

Evening Reflection

What was your walk with Christ like today?

Were you able to follow Him throughout the day?

Where did you diverge?

Did the Spirit surface any habit patterns that need to be transformed by Jesus? Are you willing?

Week 2: Day 3
Three Types of Prayerwalking

Beginnings

Bow before God and thank Him for the joy of life with Him. Open your heart to Him today to teach and lead as He chooses.

❧

Two truths regarding prayer are obvious: 1) God's Word urges us to pray at all times (1 Thess. 5:17) and 2) By and large, we don't. A survey taken of the prayer habits of 17,000 church members in the 1980s confirmed this. These believers (who were attending a "prayer for spiritual awakening" seminar at the time of the survey) averaged less than five minutes in prayer a day! The two thousand pastors and spouses present indicated they prayed less than seven minutes a day.

In 2000, George Barna concluded from a survey regarding prayer in America that the average daily prayer time was less than five minutes. There are many reasons for this, among them an incorrect understanding of what prayer really is and lack of discipline, but primarily it is an ignorance of this truth: prayer is not an option, an ornament for the well-decorated Christian life. It is to be our life.

Read Colossians 4:2. Our lives are to be devoted to _____.

Since we now understand that prayer is walking in God's presence rather than spiritual filibustering, we have crossed the threshold into the house where this biblical truth can be lived out. This is foundational to being used as prayerwalkers in the world and is known as devotional prayerwalking.

Prayer is not an option— it is to be our life.

As we walk this way through life we will no longer be just card-carrying Christians, but Christians who walk out our days in conscious realization of God's presence with us. We respond immediately to His guiding will for us and through us. We are powerful leaven in this lost world. As we walk through the normal responsibilities of our day, we are in tune with God, able to hear His voice and nod agreement, and willing to breathe a prayer of intercession for the hurting ones He brings across our path. We have become incidental prayerwalkers. We still go about our normal activities, but incidental to them we are used of God as very strategic intercessors in our world.

There is a third and very important type of prayerwalking, and it is known as intentional prayerwalking.

Read Luke 10:1. Did Christ use planning and organization skills in His ministry? Yes _____ No _____

From beginning to end, the Bible exhibits the master plan and planning of God. He is an organized, intentional God. Christ, His Son, demonstrated this same attribute in His earthly ministry. We like the excitement of the divine encounters that incidental prayerwalking often brings. Organization does not automatically preclude the epiphanic (encounters with God), it actually sets the stage for them. Something as simple as planning a time with a friend to go out and walk through your campus or community while praying for your neighbors is an example of an intentional prayerwalk. As we walk with God through our world, people encounter Him and are drawn toward Him. The kingdom of God is again, afresh, at hand.

Week 2 Day 3

Throughout Today

Consciously allow God to prompt you throughout today as an incidental prayerwalker and breathe words of silent intercession for everyone He directs you to.

Evening Reflection

How many times did the Holy Spirit prompt you to intercede for someone? For some situation? Did you?

How did God lead you to pray for them?

What fruit of the Spirit did He manifest in you as you walked with Him?

Did it visibly affect someone? How?

Beginnings

Bow before God and humbly declare to Him your willingness for Him to search you and cleanse you today. ❧

In sporting events, spectators always focus on the finish. Competitors, though, focus first on the start because they know it is critical to the finish. How we begin determines in large measure how we run and where we finish.

Read 1 Corinthians 9:24–25. How did the apostle Paul say we should run? _____

And what did he indicate was the key? _____

As followers of Jesus, we are not competitors; we are teammates. We are striving together for a common goal, and to be successful we must labor not for God, but with God. Our goal is to win, but contrary to the world's way, for us the key to winning the race is how we walk. Thus nothing is more important than nurturing our walk with God. And the key to doing this is discipline and self-control.

Nothing is more important than nurturing our walk with God.

As men and women who want to walk out a life of unhindered communion (prayer) with God, our start to each day is also critical.

Read Matthew 6:6. How did Jesus say we should begin our prayer times? _____

_____

Read Psalm 119:105. What lights the way for us and shows us how to walk? _____

During this study as you have been setting aside a private quiet time each morning to pray and read God's Word, you have been starting well today's lap in the race of life. However, you probably have already become aware of something inhibiting your fellowship with God and your effectiveness in His plan.

Read Isaiah 59:1–3. What hinders the hearing and answering of our prayers? _____

Envision a tug-of-war. On one end of the rope are Satan and his demons, dug in and resisting every effort to move them. On the other end are the children of God. As the struggle is about to begin, God makes clear what is necessary to win, and it's nothing like we've ever heard before. Instead of a pep talk including the normal clichés, "you've got what it takes," "you can do it," "pull together," "never give up," God's advice is exactly opposite. "You can't do it," He says. "Only I can. And I will only pull with you when you are prepared to pull with Me."

"We want to pull with You," we say, as we reach for the rope.

He stops us and says, "You can't put your hands on the rope."

"Why not?" we ask. "We want to pull with You."

At this He reveals the problem, "Your hands are dirty."

Sin, the stains of the world, on us and in us, precludes our laboring together with God that His kingdom may come. But before we can despair, we're reminded, "If we confess our sins, He is faithful and righteous to forgive us our sins and to cleanse us from all unrighteousness" (1 John 1:9).

Immediately we turn from every sin that He shows is hindering our fellowship and labor with Him. He cleans us up thoroughly, perfectly. Then He says, "Put your hands to the rope." Gladly, eagerly, we do it, but just before we begin to pull with all our might, He says, "Wait. There's one more thing needed before we begin."

And at that, He puts His hand to the rope.

Our Holy God in union with His holy children. Victory!

Victory begins at the start of the day with a closed door, an open Bible, and a disciplined, responsive heart ready to turn loose anything that hinders our walk and work with God for the sake of His kingdom that day.

Throughout Today

God's Spirit delights to illumine anything that is hindering our walk with Him. Determine to obey immediately. Turn loose and be cleansed and filled with that which is pure and beautiful; the very life of Christ, our Lord.

Evening Reflection

Has God revealed any hindering sin in your life today?

Was it painful to see this?

Were you resistant to acknowledging it and repenting of it?

How were you tempted to rationalize and compromise God's conviction and illumining of sin?

How does it feel to forsake sin and be cleansed and filled again with His Spirit?

Beginnings

Bow in God's holy presence and praise Him for His grace and forgiveness. Ask Him to lead you into contact with someone today that you can pray for and share with.

❧

Let's begin today by looking at 1 Timothy 2:8. How and where are we to pray? _____

As the custom in the West is to fold our hands when we pray, the Hebrews' custom was to lift their hands. Paul reiterates that as we reach out to God, it must be with hands (and hearts) cleansed from all sin. And as for location limits? There are none. We are to pray wherever we are.

Just as we must begin each day with a closed door and an open Bible, so must we follow by closing the Bible and opening the door. We can safely close our copy of God's Word because we have hidden it in our hearts. We have fed on its truth. Our souls are nourished, our spirits are refreshed, our minds are full and stimulated. We know the truth and we are set free to live it in the world. We're ready—now we're really ready—to open the door, move out, and be the church in a hurting world. And as we do we cross the threshold from petitionary (prayer for ourselves) to intercessory prayer (prayer for others). Incidental and intentional prayerwalking are types of intercessory prayer at the very sites where we are faithfully expecting God's answers.

Our intercession is never the end but the means to God's end.

Some ask, "Couldn't I just pray for the people of this town or that country right from my church or my home?"

The answer, of course, is yes. Not only can we, we must, but every prayerwalker has a testimony similar to mine and my colleagues on Main Street so long ago. Never were we so close to God and humankind at the same time as when we were prayerwalking. We identified with God and His great longing for His people and we identified with people in their great need of Him and His saving love. Additionally, they sensed that somehow the kingdom of God had indeed come near them.

We will learn all of the basic elements of on-site prayerwalking in the days ahead. This is important to remember as we move into the weekend and our first intentional prayerwalk as a group: be prepared to see people and neighborhoods as you've never seen them before. Be prepared to respond to this insight from the Holy Spirit with intercession. Be informed and enlivened.

Remember intercession is never the end but the means to God's end.

Read Mark 16:15. What did Jesus say here? _____

Jesus was very clear. We, as His followers, are to move out into all the world and share the good news of salvation with everyone. We are to go and tell. Somehow much of the church has reversed that and teaches that we are to say to the world, "Come and hear." This is neither biblical nor practical. The world isn't going to come to church. Instead, into the cocooned church that has woven walls of separation between itself and its world, comes the Spirit of God telling Christ's church to get out of the pews and even out of the prayer closets, and get back out into the world. God, through this modern movement of prayerwalking, is re-neighboring the church. And He's doing it in the most genuine and powerful way; the church is obediently and humbly walking with Him in prayer that His kingdom may finally come and His will be done in all the earth.

Throughout Today

As you move into your day, commit to be ready to see what He shows you about someone and then to instantly intercede for them in light of the insight He's given you. Be sure that you don't draw the line at just prayer. Even if you are fearful, be ready to honestly share what Jesus has done for you as God gives you an opportunity.

Evening Reflection

How did God answer your prayer today?

Who did He bring across your path as you became His church in the world?

Were you able to talk with them?

Did they share a need that you could take to God in prayer?

How did you feel about today and this week?

Insights from a Prayerwalk

A few years ago, Pastor Gary Crawford of Gainesville, Florida, went on his first prayerwalk. As he allowed the Spirit to stimulate and guide his intercession, he found all types of common sights and objects triggering pointed intercession. On the back of a piece of paper that he had in his pocket, he jotted down these everyday sights and the prayers that they elicited.

Item	Prayer that...
Basketball	people would not bounce from one fad to another
Butterfly	God would do something beautiful in the city
Lily	He would truly be the Lily of the valley
Corner windows	there would be no dark corners in the neighborhood lives and homes
Limb	Christians would risk going out on a limb with God
Rose	Christ would be the Rose of Sharon there
Playhouse	people would come out of their playhouses and go to God's house
Peaceful day	God would bring peace
Spreading branch	the gospel would spread over the city like an oak tree
Tire swing	we would trust Jesus to empower us as we do those who push a swing
Fence	we would remove fences that separate us from God; He would build a fence of protection around believers

Power lines	the power of the Holy Spirit would permeate us
Phone lines	people would have a desire to talk with God and listen to Him
Transformer	we would be transformed by the renewing of our minds
Trash can	we would remove the spiritual trash in our lives
Rake	we would tend our spiritual yards
Redbird	the blood of Jesus would cover the lives of the people in the neighborhood
American flag	people would have commitment to Christ
Tag saying "Sahara"	God would be a spiritual oasis
Locked mailbox	people would not lock out His Word sent to them
Child's toy	children would love Jesus
"Slow Down" sign	people would slow down and listen to God
Bird singing	people would sing a song of God
Black cross	people would resist the prince of darkness
Lake	Jesus would become living water to the people in the neighborhood
Sailboat	the wind of the Spirit would blow there
Lift station	the cross of Christ would be lifted up there

Third Week

Praying God's Will Into the World

"Pray, then, in this way: . . . Thy kingdom come.
Thy will be done, on earth as it is in heaven."
(Matthew 6:9–10)

<u>*This week we will:*</u>

- see how God is at work today
- recognize when God is speaking
- pray God's purposes
- pray God's promises
- speak God's blessings

Beginnings

Bow before God who loves you and gave His Son for you. Express your gratitude to Him and commit to join Him in His work of redemption.

❧

Some new missionaries told me with excitement that they couldn't wait to get to their field so that they could be "on mission for God." Their fervency was commendable but their theology was not.

Open your Bible to John 5 and read verses 17–20. Who is at work in the world? _____

_____

Yes, God is working to bring humanity to Himself. He's on a mission.

Was Jesus at work as well? _____

What distinction did He make, though, regarding His work? (verse 20) __

_____

Jesus didn't work from or by Himself but only as a co-laborer with God. In fact, Jesus went on to say, "By myself I can do nothing" (v. 30 NIV) and in John 15:5 He tells us that neither can we!

So if we can't and shouldn't be on mission for God, how are we to live? After all, He did say to us as His followers, "Go therefore and make disciples of all the nations" (Matthew 28:19).

Turn to 1 Corinthians 3:9. How are we to walk and work in this world?

_____

We are to walk in the work that God is about. God is able. We are not (2 Corinthians 3:5). God is the Initiator. We are the responders. This is always true in work that advances His kingdom and is especially true in prayer. We recognize God's work by the nature of the work. We are enabled to see it for what it is by the testimony of His Word and the illumining of the Holy Spirit. God's work is an expression of His will and His will is advanced in that work.

We commonly see God at work in two ways. 1) We encounter someone who is spiritually searching (John 6:44). 2) We sense His working in us and we respond with agreement and prayer of expectation.

When we pray in this way, we are praying His will and we have assurance from Him that when we pray this way, He hears and answers (1 John 5:14–15). And as we pray in light of and in line with what we encounter Him doing in us or around us, He is then able to advance His work at that point. While God certainly is sovereign and could do what He pleases when and how He pleases, He has chosen instead to make His work dependent upon the faithful prayers and obedient lives of His children.

God is the Initiator. We are the responders.

During your first intentional prayerwalk this past weekend, was there an area where you or one of your walking partners recognized God at work? Briefly describe it._____

_____

_____

How did you pray in light of that realization? _____

Did you realize that you were linking with God in His mission of love to a lost world and that that mission was advanced as you prayed? _____

Throughout Today

Ask God to show you where and in whom He is at work today. Ready yourself to instantly recognize His work and pray immediately in light of what you see. Then tell Him that you are ready for Him to use you in that work in any way He chooses.

Today's Prayerwalk

Beginning today and for the rest of this study, you will be participating in a brief prayerwalk each day. Normally this will be something you do alone but you certainly may walk with a fellow believer as God directs. Where are two places that you could prayerwalk for a few minutes today?

1.

2.

Choose one.

Week 3 Day 1

Evening Reflection

Where did you choose to prayerwalk today?

For whom did you pray?

What did you experience as you prayerwalked?

Did you recognize God at work in any way?

What was your response?

Week 3: Day 2
Hearing and Heeding His Voice

Beginnings

Bow and express your gratitude for God's work in your life and in the world. Ask God to tune your ear to hear His voice and your heart to receive His guidance.

❧

It happened some years ago at a prayerwalk practicum in Louisville, Kentucky. On Saturday morning the lady came to the session in tears. The night before, we had studied how God speaks to us and why. The story she related that morning was tragic.

The evening before she had been so excited about learning to prayerwalk. As she drove to the stop sign at the end of her block, she noticed a neighbor in his front yard. She had a sense that she should stop and talk with the man. But she was almost late to the practicum so she said to herself, "I'll do that later." The next morning as she was getting ready, her neighbor came over saying, "Did you hear about the man down in the corner house?" She instantly had a flashback of her earlier impression. "No, what?" "He killed himself last night."

From still small voice to booming thunder, through dreams and even donkeys, God speaks to His people. He speaks in line with His central purpose, "The Lord is . . . not willing that any should perish but that all should come to repentance" (2 Peter 3:9 KJV), and He speaks that we might work with Him in this mission of salvation. Two questions are paramount for us as prayerwalkers committed to hearing and heeding His voice. 1) Am I ready and willing to instantly obey Him? 2) How can I be sure it is God who is speaking to me?

When you encounter God at work, what is your first thought? Do you form a reason not to respond or do you find yourself willing to reach out? If rationalization or procrastination characterize your inner response, then the Holy Spirit has just shown you that the old self-centered orientation is still controlling your life. Immediately stop and repent of this, asking God to forgive you and fill you with His Spirit. Then obey.

Now read Hebrews 1:1–2. How did God speak to His people in the past? _____ And how does He speak to us now? _____

We know that Jesus has left earth and returned to heaven to intercede unceasingly for us. How does He speak to us now? Read His words in John 16:7, 13. How does Jesus now speak to us and guide us? _____

What if we are unsure that it really is the voice of the Spirit speaking? Turn to Psalm 106:13b. What was the testimony against the children of Israel? __

_____

Yes, they rushed ahead. God deeply desires that we hear and obey His voice. His speaking will always be consistent with His Word, the Bible, and He often will confirm it through His body, the church, and with providential circumstances. Beware of trying to make your thoughts into His words and your desires into His plan. Check your heart. Is it pure in its motives? Ready to respond?

Hearing God is often a result of prayerwalking, not a prerequisite.

How might the Louisville woman have applied these guides? She could have rolled her window down and spoken a word of greeting to the man. She might have asked how he was. She could have proposed stopping by the next afternoon to visit or she could have simply complimented him on the beauty of his yard. Each of these possibilities would have indicated her responsiveness to the Spirit's prompting and given God opportunity to communicate love to the man while opening a further opportunity for ministry. As she reached out she could have been praying, asking God to bless her response and guide her in the next step. God takes delight in answering and honors our obedience.

Throughout Today

Live out this fresh revelation that God is speaking to us as we walk with Him through the world. Ask Him to help you today to recognize when He does speak to you.

Also, if He has illumined any resistance in your heart this morning, bow and repent of that before you walk into your day.

Today's Prayerwalk

Yesterday you identified two places where you could prayerwalk for a few minutes and you chose one. Today, go to the other place you identified and pray there.

Expect God to guide your silent praying and respond as He does. Be ready for an opportunity to speak to someone. Remember that hearing God is often a *result* of prayerwalking, not a prerequisite.

Evening Reflection

What did you experience during your prayerwalk today?

Did God speak to you during it?

Did He speak to you during the day?

What did He say?

How did you respond?

Beginnings

Bow quietly and after some moments of stillness, allow yourself to praise God. Thank Him for the Holy Spirit dwelling within you and set your heart toward His will and purposes.

❧

No symbol is more indicative of Christianity than the cross. It adorns churches worldwide and is worn by Christians, both men and women. Is the cross to be just a symbol or does it have a practical role in our daily lives? At the end of our first week in this process of transformation into prayerwalkers, we discovered the wonderful truth that the Christian life is one of following Jesus. Now let's look at Luke 9:23 and see what is required of those who desire to come after Him. What is necessary before we can follow Jesus? _____

_____

> *Our world is grossly at cross purposes with God's desire and plan for it.*

First we must deny ourselves. This sounds simple, but it is radically counter-cultural. Throughout our lives, we are taught the pseudo-truth that rather than deny ourselves, we are to indulge ourselves. As we live this way, though, we come to recognize the enslaving power of this kind of self-centered living. In denying ourselves for the sake of walking with Jesus, our lives cease being at cross purposes, or in disagreement, with His.

From self-denial, Jesus moves on to the next essential step: taking up our cross daily. A cross has only one purpose: death. When our Lord exhorts us to take up our cross each day, He is giving us practical guidance on how to live for Him and die to ourselves. How did Paul describe his life? (Galatians 2:20)

_____

It could be said, his life was now oriented around Cross (with a capital C) Purposes, purposes of our Lord Jesus Christ. Ours are to be as well.

There are many definitions of prayer but one simple yet profound one is that prayer is surrender. We surrender our desires, our purposes, and in doing so are enabled to live and pray God's desires, His purposes. Our world is grossly at cross purposes with God's desire and plan for it. As we daily embrace a life of death to self and life in Christ, we experience the truth of Philippians 2:13. God is at work in us willing and working for His good pleasure. When we prayerwalk in the world, we are always to be praying His purposes—Cross Purposes—for the people of the world.

How may God want to will and work in you today in your world?

_____

What efforts/actions in the world do you see that are clearly at cross purposes with God's plans? _____

What are some of God's desires and purposes for His world? _____

_____

Throughout Today

Ask God to make you sensitive to everything around you today that is at cross purposes with His desires. (Be alert to anything in you that He may highlight.)

Today's Prayerwalk

Think about an area where there is activity that is not in accordance with God's will. It may be hatred of our fellow man. It may be the teaching of falsehoods. It may be unethical activity. It might be simply selfish living. Go there. Acknowledge the incongruence between God's desires and the actual reality. Then, in Jesus' name, pray God's purposes will be done in the people and the setting.

Evening Reflection

Did God show you any area of your life that was at cross purposes with His desires? Did you immediately repent of it?

What did He show you in your world today that was at cross purposes with His will? What true Cross Purposes did you pray for the people there?

Beginnings

As is now your habit, quietly bow before our loving God, thanking Him for His perfect purposes for this world and committing yourself to walk and pray in line with them today.

❧

High in the mountains of central Ethiopia, I happened upon a sight so amazing I was compelled to pull the Land Rover to the side of the road and investigate. There in a region of thin soil and harsh conditions was a small tableland covered in lush vegetables of various kinds. Walking with wonder across the field toward the busy farmer, I happened upon what I thought to be the secret: running the length of his field was a small, strong stream. However, after I talked with the farmer and complimented him on his crops, he showed me the real secret to his abundance. He had produced a simple but marvelous system of dikes and gates. Using a shovel and a few small boards he was able to open the bank of his stream at any point and turn the life-giving flow into any thirsty place. The result of his understanding and daily diligence was obvious: everywhere was life and abundance.

What God promises, He performs.

God assures us that praying according to His will brings answers (1 John 5:14–15). Too often, though, our prayers are powerless because we doubt our knowledge of His will. Open your Bible to 2 Peter 1:4. What has God given us? _____.

A promise from a person is just a statement of intent until it is fulfilled and its fulfillment is solely dependent upon the character of the person making the promise. We know that God's character is perfect and immutable (unchanging). What God promises, He performs. Why then does the intent of so many of God's promises given to us in His Word go unrealized? The fault lies not with God but with us.

Read Romans 4:20 regarding Abraham and God's promise to him. What did he do about the promise? _____

Yes, Abraham understood that faith is belief in action. When we pray the promises of God as we walk through this world we are like wise farmers, believing in the strong stream of God's promised grace and opening gateways to thirsty lives with the spade of our prayers. Prayer according to His promises is not only prayer according to His will, it is also already-being-answered prayer. The flow of promised blessing is already advancing into the land even as we pray. As followers of Jesus, every promise to us carries an assured *yes* as we ask in faith (2 Corinthians 1:20).

Throughout Today

Look at a few of these promises as you prepare to move into your day and ask God to highlight one or more for you to take to heart and pray with faith for yourself and at least one to pray for those around you. If your faith seems weak, ask Him to help. He will.

John 6:47

John 14:21

Psalm 37:4

Hebrews 11:6

Romans 10:13

James 1:5

Today's Prayerwalk

Ask God to show you where you should pray on-site today. Know that He will direct you to someone He has prepared. Taking one or more of these promises, consciously pray them for those God brings to you. Be ready to speak a word of encouragement or hope if He answers while you're praying and gives you an opportunity to talk with someone. If you're insecure about what to say, pray the promise of Luke 12:12.

Evening Reflection

What promises did God highlight to you today?

What was it like to know you were praying in God's will?

What was it like to know that He was answering as you prayed?

Week 3: Day 5
Praying God's Blessings

Beginnings

As you bow your life before Him this morning, mingle with your praise thanksgiving for the many and marvelous promises He has made to us in His Word. Invite Him to use you in a new way today.

❦

From the Garden forward, all of life has been tainted by the curse. Humans, in turn, from our fallen state, have interrelated by wishing and working ill toward others. God, in the person of the Savior, took for us the full brunt of the curse and returned to us blessing. In doing this He made it possible not only for us to receive blessing, but also gave us the privilege to bless.

An aged African was a beloved colleague of missionary Bud Fray. Serving in Rhodesia (now Zimbabwe), they labored together to take the good news to people who had never heard. They always prepared with deliberate and careful prayer before extending the kingdom to a new village that had never heard the good news. Praying for both the lost and the laborers, they would wait and pray until God gave the release to proceed. Then they would get in the Land Rover and journey to the village. Always the approach was the same. Nearing the village the old believer would ask that the vehicle be stopped. Slowly climbing out he would lay face down on the ground before God and in singular fervency speak words of blessing, saying, "Let there be light."

Our words of blessing match God's will for blessing.

God, in grace, has made us priests before Him (Revelation 1:6), and in this we have both power and privilege to bless people and the peoples of the earth. It was the common and expected practice of the children of Israel to speak blessings. "The blessing of the Lord be upon you," and "We bless you in the name of the Lord" (Psalm 129:8).

To bless in this way is to give a gift by speaking the intent of God. It is not magic as some suppose. Magic is engaging in ritualized activity to gain power or influence. Blessing is verbal engagement in God-agreement regarding His desires for people. Our words of blessing match God's will for blessing. And He honors our faithful speaking by doing that which we speak.

Jesus taught the church to approach its evangelism and kingdom extension efforts in this same way. Read Luke 10:5. What did Jesus command the disciples to speak as they entered a house? _____

Yes, His desire for those of that home—peace—was spoken as a blessing.

Lastly today, let's note an important connection. Realization of the blessing is determined by receptivity to the blessing. For the blessing to reside it must find a prepared heart. This highlights the vital importance of our praying His purposes and promises ahead of our divinely-illumined blessing. As we prayerwalk, our prayers prepare the way for God to bless, we become a blessing, and people receive a blessing.

Throughout Today

Thank God for enduing us with the power and privilege to bless. Ask Him to reveal a blessing He desires for someone you will pass today.

Today's Prayerwalk

Think for a few moments about how God led you to pray one of His promises or purposes on a past day's prayerwalk. Knowing that He has been answering your prayers of purpose and promise in the lives of those you prayed near, go back and now pray a blessing over them. You don't have to declare the blessing in a loud voice. Just speak it before God. He will honor it. The following Scriptures are good examples of biblical blessings:

Numbers 6:24–27   1 Kings 8:56–61

Evening Reflection

Was this your first time to ever bless someone? What was it like?

Did you find that you yourself were also blessed? Thank God for the joy that was yours today as you blessed others in His name. Ask Him to continue to open your eyes to His vast desires for blessing as you read His Word.

Fourth Week

Prayerwalking and Ministry in Community

KEY SCRIPTURE

"Let your light so shine before men, that they may see your good works, and glorify your Father which is in heaven." (Matthew 5:16 KJV)

This week we will:
- learn the place and power of worship in prayerwalking
- pray from heaven's perspective
- open the way for ministry
- minister through prayerwalking directly to people
- learn prayerwalking's power to take us to the hidden places

Week 4: Day 1
Ministering Through Prayerwalking Before the Heavenly Community

Beginnings

By now, bowing before Him each morning is already a pattern of your praying. As you do, thank Him that this is the case. The reverence we instantly sense as we approach our awesome and gracious Father sets the tone and direction for this week's focus on His love and work through us in community.

❦

She was an elderly retired schoolteacher embarking on her first intentional prayerwalk. Having been trained, she already knew much of what to expect as she struck out with her partner. Returning, though, it was obvious something else had happened. Her exclamation made it immediately clear, "I am in His majestic presence—right now!"

In prayer-walking our service is always first to God and then to others.

Preeminently, prayerwalking is not an activity that occurs before the earthly community but rather one that unfolds before the heavenly community. Some people, as well as all heaven, will watch as we pray but we must be resolute in our orientation: it is toward God and not the gallery that we look, and foremost in our orientation intent is giving, not getting. We give ourselves to Him and we give Him what He is worthy of—thanks, praise, worship, and blessing. How often are we to do this? (Psalm 34:1) _____

Worship, which is giving honor where honor is due, is a fruit of knowing God. Where worship is absent, it is because knowledge of God is absent. Conversely, as we know Him more, we cannot help but worship and praise Him more. You have already been experiencing this truth. Each day as you have spent time in God's Word using this book as a tool, you have learned more about Him. In knowing God's Word, you've come to know God and spontaneous expressions of gratitude and wonder have been your responses.

Although we worship God because He alone is worthy of it (in other words, our motives are pure) there is something that happens as we worship. Read Psalm 22:3. What occurs as we give Him praise? _____

Yes, God comes and inhabits, takes up residence, in the praises of His people (KJV). He is actually enthroned upon our praise (NASB). As we take prayer to the streets where God is not welcome and His presence is unnoticed, our praise becomes an entry point for His holy presence. God is suddenly present among people in His rightful position, enthroned, and whether people realize it or not, they will be affected by God, who has come near.

Look at the activity of the early church (Acts 13:1–3). Here we find the church leaders gathered, possibly with the whole congregation, and their fasting and worship is described as service. Notice then that their service to God in worship is followed by His sending them out to serve and minister to people. This biblical order is the correct order.

In prayerwalking our service is always first to God and then to others. Be assured that as we serve Him through moving praise and worship in our world today, He will be honored and people will be impacted by His presence among them.

Throughout Today

Determine to praise God today based on your knowledge of Him. Ask the Holy Spirit to illumine Scripture that proclaims who God is. Then as you move through your day, be alert to His doing this and immediately respond in praise consistent with the truth.

Today's Prayerwalk

Think about a place where God is not acknowledged or widely known. It may be the office of someone who vehemently rejects God. It may be a place on campus where the focus is ungodly. Go there and silently praise God for who He is and who He is to you.

Lift up His glories in the place, near those who do not acknowledge and give Him worship. Then, in faith, ask that they might realize His love and open their hearts to Him.

Week 4 Day 1

Evening Reflection

Remember your specific praise of God today and repeat it to Him.

Enjoy the goodness of God that the Holy Spirit revealed to you today.

Did God reveal anything new to you about Himself? What?

Week 4: Day 2
Ministry Through Prayerwalking From the Heavenly Community

Beginnings

Open your Bible to Psalm 34, which you prayed from yesterday. Quiet yourself and begin the day by reflecting upon the attributes of God contained there. Worship Him with a grateful heart and give thanks for His gracious provision in your life.

❧

The moment was a contrast in expectation. Luke recounts it in chapter 7 of his Gospel beginning at verse 11. Read the paragraph. Two crowds meet each other but their moods and outlooks are poles apart. The one, traveling out of the city, is grieving and hopeless. The other traveling into the city is excited and expectant. Each crowd is epitomized by the person at its center: in one, a devastated mother; in the other, Jesus. As the crowds pass, Jesus sees and connects with the mother. He stops and speaks to her. What does He say? _____

This phrase, "don't cry," seems strange for a woman who is now destitute. Not only is her husband dead, but in losing her only son she has lost all hope of a future. Her friends can offer no consolation. They can only weep with her. Why can Jesus' word be so different? Perspective. The mother's friends see the situation from an earthly vantage point. Jesus sees her situation from a heavenly one.

As prayerwalkers following Jesus to and among the hurting people of our world, our perspective will be critical to our empathy with them and our intercession for them. We, too, must have a heavenly perspective.

We might be tempted to say, "That's easy for Jesus. He is the Son of God. As humans, we're earth-bound."

The question we must ask is, "Are we really?"

> *In general, perspective determines response, and response determines result.*

Read Ephesians 2:4–6. Certainly we were dead in our sins but God made us alive in Christ. Now according to His Word, where has He placed us positionally? _____

Yes, we actually are seated in the heavenlies with Christ, our Lord. We can and do have a heavenly perspective from which to view and respond to the world and its heartaches. This is critical for us as world-shaping prayerwalkers because, in general, perspective determines response, and response determines result.

When we live looking at life from heaven's vantage point, we see situations and circumstances from God's perspective. We see them in contrast to His greatness and they look small and unintimidating. Faith and hope and peace and expectancy are just a few of the fruits of this look at life.

But when our look to life is earth-oriented, the challenges loom large and we are overwhelmed. As discouraging as this seems, it is not the most critical issue. The world will say to us things like, "think positive" or "remember the glass is not half-empty, it's half-full." But this is little comfort and no hope. So we look for God and find another even more distressing reality: when we look for God from this earthly orientation, He looks small and far away. And so we go back to life burdened, discouraged, pressured, anxious, and hurried. We haven't heard the heavenly words, "don't cry."

The world's advice is, "keep looking up." That's bad counsel for us as followers of Jesus. A better word would be, "keep looking down."

Throughout Today

Think of a situation that you have been viewing from the world's perspective. Ask God to forgive you for that and then turn and begin to look at it from His perspective. We do this by looking at situations through the lens of truth.

Does it seem that you are alone in a problem? "I will never leave thee, nor forsake thee" (Hebrews 13:5 KJV). Does it seem that the world is overwhelming you? "Take courage; I have overcome the world" (John 16:33). Do you not know what to do? "The Spirit of truth . . . will guide you" (John 16:13). Look to the truth and then look at the situation through the truth. You will be seeing it from heaven's perspective.

Today's Prayerwalk

Now think about a setting where you have either prayerwalked previously or where there is a need but you have not been able to pray in faith. Ask God to reveal to you truth that relates to the situation and then go there and prayerwalk today, interceding from the heavenly perspective.

Evening Reflection

Did God stretch you today? In what way?

Did you struggle at any point? Where?

If so, ask God to speak to you in the night and reveal His perspective on the situation. Then rest in Him as He guides you into truth for the question. Ready yourself to pray that truth into the situation tomorrow.

Week 4 Day 2

Week 4: Day 3
Ministry through Prayerwalking on Behalf of the Human Community

Beginnings

As you prepare to bow before Him this morning, remember your experience yesterday and the heavenly perspective that God gave you in that earthly situation. Praise Him for giving truth that transforms us and thus enables our prayer to be transforming prayer. Then invite Him to lead you to someone today that you can minister to.

❦

The single mom hurried in late for our first prayerwalk. She had attended each of the three evenings for studying the strategic activity of prayerwalking. This evening we were going out two-by-two to pray for their entire town in one evening. Most of the teams had gone when she came up to me saying, "I'm sorry I'm late, but my job held me and I had to pick up my little girl. I don't have a partner and I don't know where to go, but I really do want to go out and pray." Behind her, a lady at the map table selected one of the few remaining maps. Before I could respond, she said, "I don't have a partner, either. You can go with me." In a moment they were out the door.

Later that evening the one hundred or so people gathered in the church's fellowship hall to share with one another their first prayerwalking experience. I saw the single mom stand up. As she began speaking, the room hushed. Telling of her late arrival and God's preparation of a partner for her, she told of their drive to the area their map indicated. As they drove they prayed, committing themselves as servants of God for His purposes. Following the map, the driver turned the final corner and pulled to the curb. A choking sob came from the young mother. When she could talk, she said, "I can't pray here."

"Why not?"

Pointing down the street, she said, "That's the house where my husband lives with his mistress."

Heaven came down. The eyes of a church family filled with tears and the room filled with the precious presence of God bringing divine empathy and compassion.

"We stayed in the car a long time and I gave every reason why I could not and why I didn't have to pray there. My new friend didn't say much except to cry with me and pray for me. When I'd given every reason I could, I realized God was speaking to me. 'I brought you here,' He said."

"That was all. But that was enough. We both knew it. What else could we do? We had to get out of the car. I couldn't pray. I just let God pray whatever He wanted through me. We prayed for every house on that street."

"Tonight I was going out to pray that people in bondage would be set free in Jesus. I learned that God also wanted to set me free. I forgave my husband and the woman and I prayed for them. And tonight I was set free. I pray they will come to know this same wonderful freedom."

God wants to bring freedom from sin to all people. As prayerwalkers, we are laborers to that end. Look once more in yesterday's Luke 7 passage. Notice verse 13.

"When Jesus saw her, his heart broke" *(The Message)*. The key to genuine empathic intercession seems to be identifying with people. This is true, but only secondarily. Primarily, the key to this kind of praying is identification with God.

Jesus' life was in complete harmony with the life of God in Him. He saw and interacted with the world from heaven's perspective. In the case of the mom, though, and all of us, there are sometimes things that hinder our usefulness in God's hand. Whenever this is true, He works to rid our lives of that.

> ## *God wants to do, through us, powerful work in the lives of hurting people. For that to happen, He first must be allowed to do powerful work in us.*

God engineers circumstances to that end. All that is necessary for this cleansing, liberating work to be successful is our willing cooperation.

We give Him an unqualified welcome to do in us and with us whatever He desires. Then we are willing and useable to extend a vicarious welcome to Him on behalf of others.

Throughout Today

Today is a critical day in our transformation into genuine on-site pray-ers. God wants to do, through us, powerful work in the lives of hurting people. For that to happen, He first must be allowed to do powerful work in us. Immediately recognize this and welcome this work in us. Focus, today, on being sensitive to this work of the Spirit in us and responsive without reservation.

Today's Prayerwalk

Say to God that you are willing to go and intercede anywhere He wants you to and for whomever He wants you to. Then do it to His glory.

Evening Reflection

Honestly record whatever God said and did in you today.

Give Him thanks and praise.

Rest in His freedom tonight.

Week 4: Day 4
Ministering Through Prayerwalking
To the Human Community

Beginnings

Praise God this morning that while we were lost and wandering in the world, He came to us and, in love, brought us into His house. Thank Him for this gentle yet persevering love. Ask Him to fill you with that kind of love and then show you how He wants to reach out to someone as you prayerwalk your way through today.

❧

God's heart hurts with the hurting hearts of people everywhere, and He can take the most unlikely of situations and turn it into a bridge of love. All it takes is readiness and willingness in us.

A missionary wrote, "The people of Guatemala value prayer very highly. They consider it the highest expression of God's love." In fact, all intercession is an act of love and on-site intercession even more so because it adds the actual going to people and then reaching out to them in love. The going is love in motion and the reaching out is love in action.

In New York City, Jesus said to believers, "Follow Me out onto the sidewalks of New York and I will touch people right there, through you and your prayers, with my love." Skeptics said New Yorkers would never share their needs right on the sidewalk and they certainly would never allow strangers to pray for them in that kind of public setting. As always, when it comes to Jesus' word versus the skeptics' word, He is right every time. And He was this time. Setting up little folding tables with hand-lettered signs on them, "Prayer Station," a band of Christians in New York took their prayers to the streets. Now some years later, only God knows how many tens of thousands of New Yorkers have been touched by His love as they poured their hearts out to these on-site intercessors and then experienced God as they were prayed for.

Open your Bible to Luke 19 and read the first ten verses. Here is Jesus just passing through a place when a seeming chance encounter is turned into a divine encounter that results in salvation coming to a whole family. Notice these elements that have great significance for us each day as prayerwalkers in the world.

•There was a great crowd but God sees the "one" who is willing and needy and ready. (verses 3–5)

Application: We must be walking in-touch with Christ each day so that we, too, can see the "one" and focus on her or him.

•God sets the stage and then He reaches out in love. (verse 5)

Application: God is always the initiator and we are the responders. Be ready to respond and be the bridge.

•Our word becomes God's bridge. (verse 5)

Application: Expect that God has already initiated in the person and that they are ready to respond. Speak to them and to God on their behalf.

All intercession is an act of love.

A man stood during the closing session of a national prayer summit in the spring of 2000. In the military he had become a heavy drinker and drug user. After several years of this, he realized he was destroying his life. As God brought that realization to him, He also brought someone to him with love and the word of love. Like Nicodemus, he joyously accepted it. Now only two years into his new life in Christ, he had come to realize that God wanted to reach out to many other people in situations that seemed just as hopeless as his once did.

During a prayerwalk conference at the summit God had shown Him the incredible potential of in-the-world prayer. He was standing to testify that he was going back with a vision and a commitment to pray up and down every street in his community and intercede for the people in every house in his town. When God answered His prayers and opened doors to people, he would speak the same words of love and hope that another caring person had spoken to him. How could he possibly accomplish such a comprehensive, community-wide task? The man shared that God had given him the perfect occupation: he drove a garbage truck.

Throughout Today

God can sanctify just about any job or activity. All that is required is that we want Him to, ask Him to, and then allow Him to. As you walk into today, answer these questions:

Do you want Him to sanctify the activities of your day? Would you ask Him to? Will you allow Him to?

As your desire meshes with God's desire, as your prayer matches His will, and as you walk in step with Him, He will reach out and touch someone through you today.

Today's Prayerwalk

Ask God to reveal to you where He wants you to go today. Expect that today's prayerwalking may happen during what seems to just be a "passing-through" moment. Be alert and ready. See the one. Speak.

Regardless of how the encounter unfolds, tell the person(s) what you are actually doing. "Today I'm praying for people who live here/work here/study here/shop here." Then ask them, "Is there anything that I could pray about for you?" Sometimes people will at first be reluctant or evasive. Rest in the knowledge that this is a divine encounter and simply share a word of how much God loves them or a brief testimony of another time when someone prayed for you or you prayed for someone.

Ask again, "Is there anything that I could pray about for you?" Then be still, and let God's Spirit speak to them and listen as they begin to speak to you. Then, right there, regardless of where you are, pray out loud for them.

Evening Reflection

How did you encounter God today?

How did someone else encounter God through you today?

What did God do in them?

What did God do in you?

Respond in appropriate praise, thanksgiving, worship.

Beginnings

As believers, beginning a new day is not really starting over but picking up where we left off yesterday and moving forward with Jesus. Thank God for this continuity of life in Christ. Look back at your prayerwalking encounter yesterday. Intercede for that person again as the Spirit is impressing you. Then look ahead to today and commit yourself to follow Him wholeheartedly.

❧

Prayerwalking in south Florida, my partner and I rounded a corner and encountered a barrier across the street with a large sign that read, "Do Not Enter." The experience remains as a vivid metaphor for the countless barriers that are erected against the free flow of God's love and care to people. Most of these barriers do not carry a message this explicit, but they are just as real. Jesus, though, saw that the real barriers that had to be first overcome before God could encounter people were barriers not in people who didn't know Him, but in the very people who did know Him!

Read the last six verses of Luke, chapter 9. On the surface, what are the people saying to Jesus? _____

Yes, they seem to be saying that they will follow Jesus. What little word, though, indicates that their commitment is a qualified one? _____

God is delighted to bless others as we pray in the course of our daily activities.

The tip-off word is *but*, and although it is a tiny and common word, it reveals a major barrier in the would-be followers. "I will follow you but I want to do it on my own terms." Jesus' response makes clear that it cannot be that way. Regardless of the reason, when Jesus speaks, we are to obey. If not, we are making our wills or our wants or our ways superior to His.

In these first couple of weeks of prayerwalking we have primarily prayer-walked where we were or where we were already going. God is delighted to bless others as we pray in the course of our daily activities. (Remember incidental prayerwalking?) But as we continue to endeavor to live lives that honor and obey Him, we must expect that we will hear His voice saying, "Follow Me over there." Sometimes this is not hard, but invariably the time will come when Jesus will call us to follow Him "across the tracks" to places where we don't want to go. These are the moments that will reveal the barriers within us that hinder God doing all that He wills and wants to do through us.

In today's passage, what was the essence of Jesus' words to each of the followers who had reasons why they didn't want to obey Him explicitly? _

The supreme and orienting desire of the disciple is to please his master. Regardless of our old ways of reasoning or deciding, as children of the King, we want only to be with Him and do what He desires. This does not mean that we will become reckless or endanger our lives or the lives of others. When we follow Jesus, He is responsible for our every need. What it means is that we trust Him and we will step out on that faith whenever and wherever He leads. The word of the person in verse 57 must become our word if we are to become the kind of prayerwalkers that will let Him lead us to the hidden places of the world where people wait.

"I will follow You wherever You go."

Throughout Today

Make your first steps into this day ones of commitment to obey Him in whatever way He leads. If He reveals any barrier in you to this, ask His help as you turn loose of it in repentance and follow Him with new freedom.

Today's Prayerwalk

At an earlier time did you sense God leading you to prayerwalk somewhere that you were unwilling to go? If so, repent of that right now and tell Him that if He leads you there again, you will go.

As you pray today, ask God to show you a place that has been hidden to you where He would like you to go and intercede for the people there. It might be something as simple as the breakroom in your building or it may be as foreign to you as another part of town where people of another ethnic group live or where activities go on that you do not approve of or participate in. The important element in today's prayerwalking is that your confession truly match that of the person in verse 57: "I will follow You wherever You go."

Evening Reflection

Was this a hard day or an easy one? Why?

Is there anything that is unresolved between you and Christ regarding your willingness? Note it here.

Read again Luke 9:57–62. Ask His help and align your life with His desires.

Fifth Week

Prayerwalking
and Enemy Opposition

KEY SCRIPTURE

*"Submit yourselves, then, to God.
Resist the devil, and he will flee from you."*
(James 4:7 NIV)

This week we will:
- explore the reality of spiritual warfare
- discover the elements of the first-century church's spiritual warfare strategy
- learn the world's influence upon our walk and how to defuse it
- learn the flesh's impact upon our walk and how to counter it
- learn the devil's ways and how to resist them

Beginnings

As you quiet your spirit and focus your mind and life upon God at the start of this new week, acknowledge Him as the sovereign and omnipotent God of all the universe and of all life. Praise Him for this. Thank Him that, in Christ, the enemy has already been defeated.

❦

From its earliest steps of obedience, the New Testament church experienced both response and resistance (Acts 2). To this day the pattern remains, and the early church's response to not only resistance but to outright persecution is a model for believers of all ages.

Turn to Acts 4. When Peter and John were jailed for proclaiming the good news of salvation in Jesus, then threatened by the authorities and ordered to say not another word about Him, how did the church respond? (verse 24) _____

Faith, not fear, was their response. The church looked to God and united themselves in praise and prayer.

Read the church's prayer (verses 24–30). Who was the focus of their prayer? _____

Yes, neither their human opponents nor their spiritual enemy, Satan, are even mentioned. God was central and supreme in their praying and their practicing of the faith.

What are the only requests that the church made? (verse 29) _____
_____

The church was undeterred by the opposition. They asked God to take note of the threats but their fervent desire was that He enable them to speak the truth to the world with continuing confidence and boldness.

In the years that followed, the church continued its bold obedience, the gospel spread in every direction, and the church grew. So did opposition. And since this opposition usually came from people, a danger arose. Read Ephesians 6:12. Paul made clear that our struggle is not with _____ but actually with _____. It is vital for us as believers, and particularly as women and men who follow Jesus out into world as on-site intercessors, to remember that although opposition usually manifests itself through people, the real opposer is another. Jesus said this enemy is the devil (Matthew 13:39).

Remember in our first day of this study, we looked into the Garden (Genesis 3) and saw the account of the Fall. There Adam and Eve believed Satan instead of God and all that God intended for humankind was lost. One additional aspect of this event has critical importance for us now as we move into this week and then out into the world of spiritual struggle. Notice what preceded this awful decision and its consequences (verses 1–4). Thinking that she was countering the lie of the enemy (verse 1), Eve didn't realize that by being drawn into conversation with Satan, she was actually falling right into his cleverly-laid trap.

The enemy cannot stand or stay where there is God-focused praise.

This episode points to a dangerous practice that has found some acceptance in the modern-day church. It is that of engaging in verbal dialogue, even jousting with the enemy. This was the first step onto the slippery slope that led to the Fall and it remains just as dangerous today. The New Testament church was careful to avoid this practice and we must be too. The enemy loves and craves attention. As we keep our eyes fixed on Jesus, we not only walk in the steps of the victorious New Testament church, we reassert Christ's victory over the devil and deprive him of even our passing notice or attention.

That Satan and his minions exist and exert varying degrees of influence and opposition is biblically undeniable. Where we must be careful is in drawing our lines of belief and practice as the Scriptures do and then staying alert to the enemy's schemes to draw us across those lines. C. S. Lewis' word in his classic *The Screwtape Letters* remains a helpful word for us as practical prayer-walkers in an enemy-infiltrated world:

"There are two equal and opposite errors into which our race can fall about the devils. One is to disbelieve in their existence. The other is to believe, and to feel an excessive and unhealthy interest in them. They themselves are equally pleased by both."

Throughout Today

Make thanksgiving to Jesus the theme of today. Praise Him for faithfulness unto death to win victory over sin and death and the enemy. Celebrate that victory with unceasing praise and thanksgiving to Him.

Today's Prayerwalk

As you are responsive to the Spirit's guidance as to the site of today's on-site prayer, consider a place where the enemy has great sway and ask God if He would have you pray there. Guard your mind that even this morning's mention of the enemy does not result in a subtheme of thought about the enemy today. If that occurs, immediately resist it and consciously return to praise and worship. The enemy cannot stand or stay where there is God-focused praise.

Evening Reflection

What did you experience today as you praised Christ for His victory?

Was there any struggle for you? Did the enemy seek to hinder your praise and prayer?

How did you respond?

Close out this day by expressing your heart's feelings of gratitude to God for the life that is yours in Christ and the victory that He gives you each day.

Week 5: Day 2
Spiritual Warfare and
The New Testament Church

Beginnings

Looking to Jesus this morning with faith and gratitude, we then look to our day with confidence in Him and His power over and preparation for what we will face today. Thank God for the peace this assurance gives.

❦

While I visited the Denver suburb of Littleton (the home of Columbine High School) to lead a prayerwalk practicum for churches in the Denver area, I noticed that I could not see the Rocky Mountains. I knew they lay just west of the city and had looked forward to seeing their beauty and majesty. But despite their enormous height, I could not see them. Why? Littleton lies against the eastern base of the foothills. I knew that the mountains were right behind those foothills, but because I was so close, the foothills seemed larger than the mountains. Had I not known better, I would have assumed that they actually stood taller than the Rockies themselves. Only when I drove several miles east of Littleton and looked back west did the mighty mountains appear. Taking in their

> *All intercession is spiritual warfare.*

splendor, I hardly noticed the foothills and when I did they seemed rather to be footlights illumining the stage upon which the majesty of the mountains was displayed.

Up close in the midst of spiritual struggle, the foothills of our enemies can loom large and overwhelming. Even more dangerous is their ability to sometimes obscure the mighty mountains from whence comes our help. This is a common experience to prayerwalkers who are the advance guard of God's kingdom intentions. When this happens, we need to guard ourselves against the temptation of grasping for new ways of warring. Instead, we need to step back and regain the perspective of the biblical model.

What was the testimony of the enemies of the gospel regarding the impact of the New Testament church? (Acts 17:6) _____

Yes, despite being surrounded by an entire world permeated by evil and influenced by the enemy, the New Testament church was seen to have power sufficient to turn the world upside down. What were the central elements of their strategy? An exhaustive study of the Book of Acts reveals four that stand out as prominent.

Obviously, prayer was foundational. From the first chapter of Acts, the church is seen as continually devoting themselves to prayer (verse 14). When things were going smoothly, they prayed (3:1). When things weren't, they prayed (4:24). And as the church exploded in growth and the burden of responsibilities began to choke out their lives of prayer, the leaders quickly re-anchored themselves. "But we will devote ourselves to prayer, and to the ministry of the word" (6:4). They prayed.

From this we observe the external living of the church and see it to be a reflection of the internal lives of the church. There was no disconnect. They lived out what they prayed: truth and faith and reliance upon God. They lived out the gospel with integrity and fidelity. They lived. Acts 5, a good example of this common pattern, also includes an example of compromise and its result (Ananias and Sapphira).

When opposition became intense and insistent, the church simply stood, unmoving and unwavering. "Whether it is right in the sight of God to give heed to you rather than to God, you be the judge; for we cannot stop speaking what we have seen and heard" (4:19–20). They would not be intimidated. They stood.

The same passage points out the fourth dominant characteristic of their kingdom-advancing strategy: they spoke the truth into their world. When a count is taken of the times that each of these elements is exhibited by the early church, this one is far and away the leader. The church understood that the gospel "is the power of God unto salvation" (Romans 1:16 KJV), and they spoke the truth into lives and situations, trusting God to bring victory. And He did. They proclaimed.

Praying, living, standing, proclaiming.

There are a few incidents of direct demonic encounters in Acts but they were either incidental to other gospel ministry (5:16, 8:7, 19:12) or reactive responses to direct encounters with demonized persons (13:8, 16:16). Never once did the early church in its kingdom-expanding obedience exhibit any proactive initiative against the devil or his forces. They gave no time or attention to the enemy. Out of an unceasing walk of faithful prayer and God-centered dependence, they lived out and spoke out the transforming truth of the gospel. The entrenched forces of darkness were forced to flee and the liberating light of the gospel came in. In those rare instances when they were confronted with direct demonic opposition, they simply commanded the demons in Jesus' name to come out, and they did. Biblically, spiritual warfare has at its heart faithful Christian living and faithful Christian proclaiming.

All intercession is spiritual warfare. To intercede for others is to contend with the enemy for them. Prayerwalking is invasionary intercession. We are actually moving into enemy-held territory and so we must understand that to intercede on-site is to engage the enemy. Critical to our success is keeping our eyes focused on Jesus and not allowing them to be diverted to the would-be usurper.

The twenty-first-century church can do no better than follow the biblical model of the first-century church. And as we do, the results will be the same: the kingdom will come and His will will be done.

Throughout Today

Go into today rejoicing in the reality that God has already given us, in Christ, everything necessary for living the Christian life in godliness and victory. Determine to walk into the opportunities of this day in this reality.

Today's Prayerwalk

Following up on a previous prayerwalk or moving into a new area, review the four elements of the New Testament church's model and reflect those in your own on-site praying. Note how the Spirit leads as you walk and pray.

Evening Reflection

As you reflect back on the four elements of the early church's model, are there any that you have neglected in your life? Which ones? Ask the Lord's forgiveness and commit to integrate any missing ones into your daily life.

Week 5: Day 3
Prayerwalking and the World

Beginnings

At the midpoint of this week of study in basic spiritual warfare for prayer-walkers, you—no doubt—have already experienced evil activity in your life. This morning let's begin by declaring the preeminent place of Christ Jesus as Lord over all, including every detail of our lives. Praise Him.

❧

Now let's begin these next three days of study by opening our Bibles to Ephesians. In chapter 2 verses 1–3, Paul gives a concise outline of the three primary forces at work around us as we endeavor to faithfully follow Jesus. Then in chapter 6 verses 10–18, we find a thorough plan for our success in this struggle.

What is the first force that Paul illumined? (Ephesians 2:2) _____

Yes, it is the world. When Adam and Eve chose to reject God and His truth and believe the tempting lies of the enemy, not only did they fall but our world became a fallen place as well. This context, this environ, in which we now have our being is a fallen place in which sin and the rebellion that it represents taint everything. Each day believers and non-believers alike encounter pressures to resist God and His plan for them and instead conform to the ways of this world.

Certainly the world is impersonal, but it is important to remember that it does not operate independent of persons. If a business is characterized by deceptiveness, the business is not deceptive, its people are. If an institution is characterized by dishonesty, it's not because the institution is inherently dishonest. Its people are. Paul also makes clear that this is how we, too, formerly walked. But not any more. Now we not only have the power and the weapons to live victoriously in the midst of this oppositional world, we also have the privilege and responsibility of interceding for others that they, too, might be liberated from its power.

Read chapter 6, verses 10–18. What is the purpose of the armor? _____

_____

Yes, not only here in Ephesians but throughout the New Testament the theme in spiritual warfare is resisting the evil one and his schemes. The six parts of the armor given here are all essential and operate in an integrated and complimentary fashion toward this goal of standing firm against the enemy. Two of them, though, are especially relevant to our successful struggles in the world. They are the belt of truth and the breastplate of righteousness.

Truth shows the lie of the world and its ways. It is significant that Paul associates truth with the belt which was put on first, before the rest of the armor. Practically, as we move into the world, we too must first put on the truth of God if we expect to stand firm and faithful. Putting truth first, we will then be able to recognize even the subtleties of the worldly deception and thus put ourselves on the path to reject them.

Righteousness means good, pure, upright. We were created this way (Ecclesiastes 7:29) but it was lost in the Fall. Now no one is righteous (Romans 3:10). But Jesus has given His own righteousness that is ours as we receive it in faith (Ephesians 4:20–24) and turn, moment by moment, from unrighteousness to right thinking and living (1 Timothy 4:7).

The association of righteousness with the breastplate is very significant. The breastplate protects the heart and the other vital organs. In the same way, righteousness protects the very heart and life of believers. Put on Christ's righteousness. Live uprightly and your heart will be protected from impurity and the poison that it is.

> *Throughout the New Testament the theme in spiritual warfare is resisting the evil one and his schemes.*

Throughout Today

Consciously start your walk into the world today with an acknowledgment before God of His truth and your commitment to live in light of it.

Ensure that righteousness characterizes your life. Is there any area that the Spirit has illumined where you are not releasing a sinful attitude or activity and asking Christ to forgive you and cleanse you?

Today's Prayerwalk

Ask God to show you a place or a person where the power of the world to conform is having success. Go there and intercede for that person or those in that place, interceding in light of truth that directly confronts the deception there. Be sensitive to respond and pray as Christ guides your thoughts and perceptions.

Evening Reflection

Did you find yourself harassed or hindered today as you lived out these spiritual warfare realities? If so, in what way(s)?

What truth did the Holy Spirit give to you to confront this attack upon you?

How were you led to intercede as you took today's prayerwalk?

Week 5: Day 4
Prayerwalking and the Flesh

Beginnings

Quieting your mind and heart this morning may be difficult because of spiritual struggles, even direct attacks of the enemy. Taking the truth of Psalm 31:14–15, confess, "You are my God. I trust in You." And acknowledge, "My times are in Your hands."

❧

Returning to Ephesians 2, let's look at verse 3. What is the powerful force that Paul mentioned here? _____

It is the flesh, our sinful nature, that we all formerly followed and obeyed. The "flesh" is our inner rebellious nature that is in opposition to God and ever leans toward selfish will and action. It too, like the world, is impersonal but it never operates independent of persons. Movies aren't lustful, people are. In unbelievers this fleshly, sinful nature guides and controls the life. In us, it lives (and wars) to regain some measure of its former place and power.

As we walk in the Spirit, our fleshly nature seeks to exert its power, diverting our thoughts, challenging our obedience, offering tempting compromises, ever resisting our resistance. In other words, inner struggle for the spiritual focus and tenor of our lives is unceasing.

As we walk in the Spirit, our fleshly nature seeks to exert its power.

Looking again to Ephesians 6, we find two more of the pieces of the armor particularly important in this area. The armor is also vital as we strive to live life victoriously as a holy prayerwalk with God.

The first piece of armor refers to "having shod your feet with the preparation of the gospel of peace" (verse 15). Paul indicated in 2:3b that one of the two ways our inner sinful nature manifests itself is in our "indulging the desires of the flesh." The shoes for the warrior readied him for quick, sure movement whenever he was challenged or attacked. Before we came to Christ, wrath characterized our relationship with God and others. But when the gospel became ours, peace supplanted that wrath. No longer is enmity against God our central, controlling orientation. Peaceful cooperation is. Now each day as we ready ourselves to walk, we can make the good news of peace our vehicle.

The other is the "helmet of salvation." Paul went on to say (in 2:3b again) that the other way that cooperation with the flesh exhibits itself is in "indulging the desires . . . of the mind." The helmet obviously is designed to protect the head, the center of thought. When Paul linked the helmet with salvation and included it as a vital part of our armor for resisting evil and standing firm in the faith, he was showing us that we have all we need. Our new life in Christ, with all of its liberating and transforming realities, is more than sufficient to guard our minds. In fact, in salvation, we now have the mind of Christ (1 Corinthians 2:16). Willingly allowing His mind to think and guide our lives, we are assured of walking and warring victoriously.

Throughout Today

Be especially conscious of your thoughts and your steps today. Ask God to illumine in you any areas where you are not thinking or living as He would have you to. Be careful to adjust your life today at any point where you become aware of the flesh endeavoring to exert itself.

Today's Prayerwalk

With new insight into the ways that the flesh guides a life, ask God to show you a place where or a person for whom He desires you to intercede today. Go there and pray in light of your knowledge of the power which the flesh holds and exerts. Specifically intercede, asking that the liberating power of the gospel be brought to fruition in the life.

Evening Reflection

In what ways did you experience the flesh's efforts to direct your thoughts and actions today? How did you respond?

How did you apply the realities of the shoes of the gospel and the helmet of salvation?

Week 5: Day 5
Prayerwalking and the Devil

Beginnings

Rejoice in the reality that Jesus, our Savior, has conquered sin and death and the devil. Consciously declare the truth that you are in Christ and reaffirm that the enemy cannot touch you unless Jesus permits it or, God forbid, you open the door by sin. Praise and thank Him.

❦

As we look one more time into Ephesians 2:2, we will see the third force working in our world to lead people away from God. How did Paul describe him here? _____

He is described as the ruler of the kingdom of the air and the one who is at work in those who are disobedient. From Jesus' explanation of the parable of the tares in Matthew 13:36–39 we know that this is the enemy, the devil.

In contrast to the world and the flesh which are impersonal, the devil is both personal and direct in his evil operations. And contrary to some thought, his realm of operation is not that of structures or places or circumstances. His realm of operation is the human realm. He welcomes the world and the flesh as avenues for his efforts but he works in and through humans, via their consent and complicity, to enslave them and negatively impact and influence others.

Satan particularly hates those who love God and desire to live lives not only of holiness but cooperation with God to see His kingdom of light spread to all people. It is important to note that he actively works to keep the lost from knowing God (2 Corinthians 4:4) while accusing Christians before God, seeking permission to attack us (Job 1–2).

The two remaining pieces of armor are especially appropriate for personally reasserting Christ's victory over the devil each day in our lives. The first is the shield of faith (Ephesians 6:16). Paul explicitly states that faith is our protection and defense against the burning ordinance the enemy periodically directs our way. Faith in God is this unfailing shield because it practically declares that we are depending upon Him to keep and protect us. And He cannot fail.

The last piece of the armor is the only weapon, the sword of the Spirit which is the Word of God (6:17). All the other pieces provide protection. This one provides the offensive capability which puts the enemy to rout. The clearest example of this Word/weapon at work is found in the account of Jesus' temptation in the wilderness (Matthew 4:1–11). Each lunge of the enemy is parried and repulsed by a relevant counterthrust of Scripture. Doing the same will ensure victory in our lives.

Although it now would seem that Paul was finished presenting everything needed for successful spiritual warfare, he wasn't. Standing apart from the metaphorical mix of the armor is one last essential activity. What is it? (6:18–19) _____

The enemy cannot touch you unless Jesus permits it or, God forbid, you open the door by sin.

An unceasing life of prayer, illumined and energized by the indwelling Spirit of Christ, not only assures victory, it empowers those who proclaim the way of victory, and it ensures that liberating victory comes to those who are yet trapped in the snare of sin. Prayerwalkers are just this kind of warrior.

Throughout Today

It is vital that we keep ourselves from all sin, since to do otherwise is to open the door to the devil and give him opportunity. Ensure that no known sin has a hiding place in your life. Then walk into this day with confidence in God to protect you and use you to advance His kingdom.

Today's Prayerwalk

Has there been a place or area where you have sensed God directing you to go and pray on-site? Ask Him if He would have you stop by there today and intercede.

If not, be sensitive to the possible directing of His Spirit to someone in the trap of sin and pray for them, asking His merciful work in their hearts and minds.

Evening Reflection

What did you experience today as you walked in the Spirit?

Did you experience any efforts of the enemy to thwart or attack you? If so, what was it like? How did you respond?

Thank God for His victory in Christ in your life.

Sixth Week

Prayerwalking that All the World May Know

KEY SCRIPTURE

"Ask of Me, and I will surely give the nations as thine inheritance, and the very ends of the earth as thy possession." (Psalm 2:8)

<u>*This week we will:*</u>
- explore ways to incorporate prayerwalking into your church
- discover ways to project intercession into your community
- consider comprehensive prayerwalking for your city
- see our place in praying for the whole world
- discover the culminating aspect of prayerwalking

Week 6: Day 1
Prayerwalking and Your Local Church

Beginnings

Entering this last week of study in *Follow Me*, reflect for a moment on how God has transformed you through this study, and bow and give Him thanks. Then invite Him to show you this week how He wants to use you and your friends as strategic prayerwalkers in your community and in the world.

❧

Traveling across our nation, a common lament I hear from too many pastors concerns the deadness of midweek prayer services. Prayer is replaced by talk about prayer, and once vibrant meetings that were characterized by fervent intercession have now degenerated into "organ recitals." The handful of people present spend the time reciting, in lengthy detail, the condition of Mrs. Jones' liver and Mr. Smith's gall bladder.

While this situation is deplorable, it is not hopeless. Church leaders in tune with our infinitely creative God are discovering marvelous ways to integrate on-site praying into the everyday life of their churches and seeing prayer, in general, revitalized among their congregations.

One pastor asked those of his congregation who were coming to church prayer meeting to leave home thirty minutes early. Committing themselves as God's servants to use as He chose, they agreed to stop somewhere along their route to church and go up to a house or two. Introducing themselves to the residents, they were simply to say, "We're on our way to prayer meeting at Grace Community Church and wondered if there was any need that we could pray about for you?" They were surprised to find that total strangers were willing to share pressing needs such as a child in trouble at school or a husband whose company had been downsized, leaving him without a job. The pastor related that before long, prayer meeting was "out of control" as members shared the needs they'd discovered and exhorted one another to prayer. A little later they began to see strangers in their Sunday services and found that they were the very people that they had been praying for!

Another church sent postcards to all the homes in a neighborhood, alerting people that prayerwalkers would be praying in their area the next Wednesday evening about 7:00 p.m. They were asked to call the church office

Once vibrant meetings that were characterized by fervent intercession have now degenerated into "organ recitals."

with prayer needs or watch for the prayer-walkers. When they arrived people were watching for them. Not only were the prayers able to pray with several families, they led two people to receive Christ as Savior.

In Alabama, a church sends pairs of prayer-walkers out every Wednesday evening. Each team goes to the same blocks of homes every week so they become known by the people there. They learn names and needs. They pray for every home and increasingly are able to pray personally with residents. Neighbors eagerly await their return to share specific prayer needs. In addition, those of the congregation who are not able to go out either prayerwalk the halls of the Christian education building in preparation for Sunday school the next weekend, or gather in the prayer room to intercede for those out on the streets right then.

In Oklahoma, a church always asks everyone, as they register them for their free medical/dental clinic, if they have any prayer needs. A special prayer group, formed just to intercede for these people, then follows up with them.

Another congregation in Missouri sent prayerwalkers out into every neighborhood around their church in preparation for their upcoming Vacation Bible School. Upon return, one older gentleman who had just gone on his first prayerwalk remarked with deep emotion to the group, "I realized as I prayed from house to house that my prayer may have been the only prayer ever prayed for the salvation of that person. And that prayer may determine the eternal destiny of that soul."

God wants to make Spirit-illumined prayer in our world an integral part of every campus ministry and every outreach of the church. He will do that as we ask Him to show us how He uniquely wants to do that in our setting and as we commit ourselves to be a praying and a prayerwalking church. (By the way, enrollment at the Missouri church's vacation Bible school shot up from 66 to 253 by the week's end, and a dozen of the older children accepted Jesus as their Savior.)

Throughout Today

Ask God to show you how He wants on-site prayer to pave the way for loving ministry by and through your church. Note how He answers you. Share it with your pastor or church prayer leaders.

Today's Prayerwalk

Through today's study, has God given you a new idea for praying on your campus or in your community? Consider going there today and prayerwalking. Or it might be that you sense Him asking you to walk with Him in a neighborhood and just let Him show you what He sees there. Go with Him on this "immersion prayerwalk" not speaking out, just seeing as He immerses you in the community.

Evening Reflection

Has this been an exciting day as God has expanded your horizons? If so, how?

Has God shown you one or more ways that He wants on-site prayer to become a part of your church's ministry? List them.

Week 6: Day 2
Prayerwalking and Your Local Community

Beginnings

With anticipatory joy because of God's revelation of some of His desires for your church yesterday, begin today with thanksgiving. Then ask Him to help you lift your eyes as today we look to the fields that are our own cities and towns and begin to see ways that we, as prayerwalkers, can shape them according to God's desires.

❧

When a group of believers who have been with Jesus pray with His fearless single-mindedness, it will not be long before they are out in their community and affecting every area of community life. Remember the first-century church and the account we studied in Acts 4? Immediately, the place where they were gathered was shaken and from then on every place they went was shaken!

When we pray, we are putting on public record our agreement with God's desires for this needy world and we are asking in the answer-assuring name of His very Son. Then, we not only know that He will answer; when He does, He will receive all the credit and thus all the glory.

Where in your city or community are things not as they are in heaven? (Matthew 6:10) _____

In Virginia, a group of concerned Christian moms began meeting every Friday morning in the parking lot of their local high school. Parking their cars, they climbed into one of the women's van. On-site at the high school, every week they stood against the evil one's activities in the school and prayed down God's best for the whole school community. At times, administration even sent urgent prayer requests out to the van.

City council direction and decisions were not God-honoring. Intercessors began to attend the council meetings, sitting quietly in the back and listening, observing, and then intervening silently by prayer in line with God's desires. Atmosphere and actions began to change for the better as the group continued to pray.

The neighborhood around a church in San Diego was experiencing so much crime and so many drive-by shootings that members were afraid to attend. The church was about to die. Some counseled a move. Seeking God, they instead stayed and countered the drive-by shootings with drive-by praying. The shootings stopped and the church now has a vibrant ministry to many of the very same people who were perpetrating the crimes.

In North Carolina, the churches of one county banded together to practice what they called "Prayer at the County Gates." Setting up along each of the highways leading into the county, on-site pray-ers would put out their lawn chairs for two-hour prayer shifts during which they interceded for their county and everyone entering it. As people drove past, they saw their sign: "You were just prayed for."

When we pray, we are putting on public record our agreement with God's desires for this needy world.

Upon seeing the sign, one man turned around and came back. He was devastated by problems. The roadside intercessors, praying silently, listened as he poured out his struggles. Then they shared the hope that was within them and that day that man left the prayer station a new man in Christ.

Another day a lady came into the county to settle legal matters related to her husband divorcing her. She was weeping so hard when she left she actually got on the wrong (right?) road out of town. She saw the pray-ers with their sign. Stopping, she began to sob out her story. They held her hand, talked with her, and helped her re-ignite her relationship with Christ to the point that she left the intercessors literally leaping in liberation.

Other ways to pray for your community? Law enforcement intercession. Obtaining the names of every police officer in town, each intercessor from one church "adopted" one for regular prayer. In addition, they covenanted to pray for all law enforcement personnel each time they passed a police car.

School-zone praying. Every locality slows traffic down in school zones. Sensitized intercessors use the school zone signs and the increased time to pray for each school they pass.

Siren prayer. Every time an ambulance or fire truck siren is heard, it becomes the trigger for instant intercession for those involved in the situation.

And on and on.

Christ wants His church to touch this world at every point and turn people toward Him. Preeminently, prayerwalkers are the ones on call and ready to do just that.

Throughout Today

Thank God for the incredible privilege that is ours to shape our world and change its direction through on-site community prayer. Pray for believers throughout our nation and world to become sensitized to this enormous opportunity.

Today's Prayerwalk

Choose a community organization or entity where you have never been before. Go and intercede for those who work there.

Evening Reflection

Where did God lead you today?

How did He impress you to pray?

What kind of experience was this?

Beginnings

Thank God for the oneness with Him that is yours because of Christ. Worship Him in holiness and see with eyes of faith a coming day when worshipers are found in every part of your city or town.

❦

This morning let's look to Jesus' prayer as found in John 17. What does He indicate (verse 21) is essential if the world is to believe in Him?

_____

Unity among Christ's disciples is essential to not only answered prayer (Matthew 18:19) but also belief by an unbelieving world. Jesus taught and prayed this vital truth and the early church lived it (Acts 1:14). Today we are seeing it lived out in marvelous new ways as the wider church of Jesus Christ unites in wide-scale comprehensive intercession for whole towns and cities.

Intercessors find their hearts bound more closely not only with God but with the people in this area.

In Purcell, Oklahoma, it had been the custom of the pastors of the ministerial alliance to meet each year on the National Day of Prayer and pray together in one of the churches. Roy Lucas, then a pastor there, had recently been to a prayerwalk practicum and suggested that they instead divide into pairs and take their prayer to the streets.

Drawing up a quick plan, they moved out into the community, entering and praying at every business and office. Both the police chief and the fire chief gathered their employees when they learned what the pastors were doing. City hall stopped and gathered to be prayed for.

One team almost walked by a law firm, but instead responded to strong leading of the Holy Spirit and went in. When they told the receptionist why they had come she gestured toward the conference room and said, "Well, I guess it's good that you're here because it will take a miracle to resolve that dispute."

Listening, they could hear an intense argument going on in the room. Bowing before God, they asked His wisdom to be given and peace to prevail. An hour later the pastors were gathered at one of the churches to debrief and praise God when the receptionist rushed in. Out of breath she said, "I've been looking in every church in town for you. The only thing I know to say is 'amazing!' Right after you came in and prayed, the conference room became quiet and everything fell into place."

In Russellville, Arkansas, seven churches of different denominations came together for seven weeks of concerted prayer for their entire area. They drew an eighty-mile circle around their community and each Sunday afternoon, intercessors from all the churches got in their cars and made the eighty-mile prayer drive. They then gathered at a different church to pray together. On the last Sunday, more than two thousand gathered in the town's coliseum for a great service of united prayer and praise.

A missionary team living in a megacity in Asia has divided the entire city into grids. Each week they have their team meeting on the streets of their city. Gathering at a prearranged place in a different grid each week, they not only maintain the unity of life and purpose as a team, they are steadily and systematically praying for their entire city.

A church in Richmond, Virginia, invites other churches as they gather every September and January and send prayerwalk teams to every one of the fourteen schools in their area. They do this as a unified effort to intercede for the faculty, administration, and students at the beginning of each semester.

In Casper, Wyoming, intercessors have made the commitment to prayerwalk weekly in a growing part of the city where a new church needs to be planted.

And in many cities around the world, prayer leaders have divided cities into segments and individual churches or intercessors have taken intercessory responsibility for the segments. These kinds of unified, concerted prayer bring both personal and corporate results. Intercessors find their hearts bound more closely not only with God but with the people in their area. Churches discover God's vision and heart for their city and adjust their corporate lives to His desires.

God wants so to reach out and touch the hurting of your city. He does that through those who walk close to Him. A general model that He has blessed in countless places has two basic elements: steady, regular intercession by a smaller group of intercessors who clearly have a burden and call to this ministry augmented by occasional large scale "blitzes" of intercessors. (These occasional prayerwalkers should receive brief basic training before being sent out. The training outline on page 97 may be used for this.)

Throughout Today

Recognizing God's great heart for the people of your city or town, ask Him to show you and your church how He wants to unite His people in your place in large-scale, long-term prayer that His kingdom may come there.

Today's Prayerwalk

One of the options for your first immersion prayerwalk earlier this week was a "looking" walk with God. Today consider a "listening" walk with Him. Still your mind and soul with quiet praise and then walk with Him and allow Him to do the talking.

Evening Reflection

How did God speak to you today?

What did you do in response?

Thank Him and rest in His peace.

Week 6: Day 4
Prayerwalking to the Peoples of the Earth

Beginnings

Thank God that He so loved the whole world that He sent His precious Son to earth to be the Savior of all people. Thank Him for your salvation and for the privilege of being given, with all believers, the ministry of reconciliation.

❧

In the mid-'70s as a young missionary to Africa, I thought missionaries opened the closed places of the world. I came to understand that I was mistaken. Missionaries don't open the closed places of the world. Intercessors do.

From the day Jesus gave His Great Commission to the church, the kingdom of God has advanced across the face of the earth. Now we see in every quarter of the earth the obvious evidences of God's Spirit moving. We hear a steady stream of testimonies of the coming of His kingdom among more and more peoples who, until now, had not had the opportunity to hear the good news. This great turning to Christ has not happened in a vacuum. It is coming as a result of the greatest movement of prayer in the history of the world. The Spirit of prayer, it seems clear, is upon the earth as never before.

This reality reflects a greater reality. God is the Author of all prayer and when He calls His people before Him to ask in large and mighty faith, it is because He desires to answer in equal measure. His true heart desire is that none should perish (2 Peter 3:9). To this end, God is calling out intercessors to go to the peoples of the earth and the ends of the earth in fervent, Spirit-illumined intercession to prepare the way of the Lord. Are you willing to go if He calls you?

After a major evangelistic campaign in Chad, Christian workers went back and compared areas where the people eagerly responded to the gospel with those where they did not. They found that the areas of response were the very ones where prayerwalk teams had been sent in advance.

In a Muslim area where workers were distributing New Testaments and *Jesus* films, they discovered that when they prayed as they walked and worked, people received the materials. When they did not, the people refused.

On-site prayer prepares the way of the Lord.

It also changes the people of the Lord. In Colombia, a prayerwalking missionary wrote, "I had wanted to see what God wanted to do in others. He chose to show me what He wants to do in me."

A church in Oklahoma discovered that an overseas prayer journey brings change both there and back home. "We came back with a renewed interest in our own city. Also, our Wednesday night prayer meetings have changed dramatically. We've also baptized more people since returning than in any other time period."

Many prayer journeys to other countries are part of strategies for a specific people group. Some, though, involve whole nations. Even continents and restricted access countries are not excluded. In fact, when prayerwalkers could not enter Libya to live out their burden and passion for the people of that nation, they simultaneously sent teams to every surrounding country. These teams moved up to the borders and literally encircled the nation with prayer as they looked across into the land.

Missionaries don't open the closed places of the world. Intercessors do.

As this book is being released, the largest prayerwalking initiative in history is underway: 2001 PRAY (Pray 'Round Africa—Yes!). Christians in every nation of that great continent are receiving prayerwalkers from all over the world. Together they will prayerwalk throughout their respective countries. On August 3, 2001, a great and fragrant incense of intercession rose from the entire continent as hundreds of thousands of intercessors knelt together and asked God to pour out His mercy and grace on the people of the entire continent.

Christian missionaries of every persuasion are requesting both prayerwalking teams and combination teams such as medical/prayerwalking and construction/prayerwalking. Missionaries have realized that when a volunteer uses his hands to build a church, he builds a church. But when he uses his hands with prayer, he builds the Church. Your minister can put you in touch with a missionary or a mission agency that wants prayerwalkers to come to the fields of the world. Ask. Seek. Knock.

And go, as God directs.

Throughout Today

Pray, without ceasing, for the kingdom to come in all the earth. Confess either your reluctance to go as an overseas prayerwalker and ask God's forgiveness and help, or your willingness to go wherever He leads.

Today's Prayerwalk

Is there an area of your town where people from another nation live? Ask God if you might go there and intercede. Be ready to not only pray as He directs but to respond as He might lead. Pray also for your church that they would be willing to join God in going beyond your Jerusalem to the Judeas, Samarias, and uttermost parts of the earth.

Evening Reflection

How did God open your life to the lost of the world?

How did He speak to you regarding your place in advancing His kingdom throughout the entire earth?

How have you responded?

Week 6 Day 4

Week 6: Day 5
Prayerwalking to the Ends of the Earth
And the End of the Age

Beginnings

On this last day of study, reflect on the major ways God has transformed you. Note them. Then humbly bow and give Him thanks. Commit to follow Him, in prayer, into the world, for the rest of your earthly days.

❧

Two givens illumine this last step that we are about to take. They are: 1) There have always been children of God who have prayed as they walked through life, and 2) Accepting that truth, there is no doubt that in the last quarter of the twentieth century, God began to do something unique and enormous in and with as-you-go, in-the-world prayer. These two are beyond dispute. A third element is also present and it perhaps has the greatest significance. It is the eschatological.

This big word refers to "last things." Old Testament eschatology looks forward with the twin themes of hope and promise. New Testament eschatology continues these as subthemes, but under a primary focus of fulfillment. What God promised and humans long for has been fulfilled in Jesus.

Read Mark 1:15. What does Jesus say regarding the time of anticipating His coming? _____

And regarding the coming of the kingdom? _____

Yes, the time has been fulfilled and now the long-hoped-for kingdom of God has come.

How does Jesus teach us to pray regarding the kingdom of God? (Matthew 6:10 _____

Indeed, here we find Him teaching and exhorting us to pray that the kingdom would come.

So the question facing us is has the kingdom come or is it yet to come? The answer is yes!

This is one of those topics that has both a present and a yet-to-be realized character. God has come to set all people free from sin and death. In that sense the kingdom of God has come. Jesus died, paying the penalty for our sin and now we have become reconciled to God.

But there is also the future characteristic. Not only are we reconciled, we also have been made ministers of this reconciliation. In this God-given mission ("Go into all the world and preach the good news to all creation," Mark 16:15 NIV), we must go and share this offer of infinite value. "Come to Me, all who are weary and heavy-laden, and I will give you rest" (Matthew 11:28). Person by person as the offer is received, the kingdom of God is spread ever more fully through the earth.

There are, however, two major problems. We do not have the power to successfully complete this privileged assignment. And the people of the world do not want what we have to offer.

Provisions for both have been made by God and their appropriation is found in the life/walk of prayer. By a life of unceasing petition, we appropriate everything necessary for life and godliness. It was all given in Christ and it becomes ours as we ask and receive.

> ## *The praying church is the kingdom come. The prayerwalking church is the kingdom coming.*

In a life then characterized by the following of Jesus throughout each day, we find our lives increasingly characterized by loving, fervent, illumined, faith-full intercession. And those of the world who need God's saving love but resist it, slowly change before our very eyes. The Spirit, in answer to our Christ-guided prayers, softens hard hearts, opens blinded minds, breaks off the enemy's shackles, and turns the will from resistance to wanting. Then when the word of reconciliation is spoken, it is a word already desired and willingly received. In another life, His will has been done and His kingdom has come.

Turn to Matthew 24:14. In probably the most explicit eschatological passage in the New Testament, what does Jesus say must happen before the end comes? _____

Before the end of the world can come, this kingdom-bringing word, the good news, must be shared with all peoples (that's what the word *nations* means here). From Revelation 7:9 we know that people from every one of these people groups will believe the Word and be born again. God's kingdom, His effective rule will have been extended to all the earth. Then at His chosen time, He will end this age.

The praying church is the kingdom come. The prayerwalking church is the kingdom coming. This is the glorious culminating aspect of prayerwalking. Christ leads the prayerwalkers out to the last enemy-held strongholds of the earth and captives are set free. Press on. Pray on. We see the kingdom coming.

Maranatha!

And Hallelujah!

Throughout Today

Let praise overwhelm and dominate your every thought and prayer today.

Today's Prayerwalk

Make today's prayerwalk, regardless of where you go, one of glorious forward-looking faith and kingdom-bringing intercession.

Evening Reflection

Let the greatness of God's love buoy you as you rest in Him.

Let His thoughts be yours and thank and praise Him as they come.

Commit, with joy, to walk with Him forever.

How Can I Become a Prayerwalker?

Preparing to Walk

1. Recognize that God is calling you to join Him in prayer in the world. Say yes!
2. Stay prepared to walk with Him by confessing any hidden sin and then by keeping your life pure.
3. Read and meditate on the Word of God daily. His Word will increasingly frame your prayers in perfect accordance with His will.
4. Invite the Holy Spirit to fill you and guide you daily.
5. Be ready to obey Him whether He leads you to another neighborhood or another country.

Stepping Out

1. Keep your eyes and ears open. Be alert and respond in prayer.
2. Listen, then speak. Feel free to pray silently and aloud. Praise Him and worship as you walk.
3. Go with a partner or two.
4. Move slowly so that God may move fully in and through you.
5. Claim God's promises. Bless the people around you. Ask of God His greatest desires for them.
6. Anticipate the devil's interference and even harassment. Resist him, firm in your faith, and continue moving forward under the protection of God.
7. Expect God to answer your prayers. Be ready to share a word of greeting and encouragement to those you meet as well as a witness to the hope that is within you.
8. Tell people that you are praying for them and their neighborhood and ask them if there is any need that you could bring to God for them. Pray right then with them.

Final Thought

Remember: Never do we accomplish more, quicker, than when we're praying.

Facilitator's Guide

Because you have turned here to the facilitator's guide, I know that you are interested in and open to helping a group of pray-ers move through the *Follow Me* experience that Jesus might transform them into prayerwalkers. Thank you.

You might have expected to find a leader's guide here instead of this facilitator's guide. Why facilitator? Because facilitate means "to make easier." A leader shows the way. A facilitator prepares the way. Jesus will be leading out in this experience and showing the way, each day. You will be who you are: a chosen vessel to make the journey easier. Christ has brought you to this vital position that He might work through you to prepare the way for the new truths and experiences that the participants will have in each new week, and to help them in understanding the significance of what they've experienced as they incorporate it into their new way of walking and living.

This guide will provide you the framework and the elements of the weekly group meeting that will enhance these purposes being achieved. Additional resources are listed on the Resources page.

Groups

It is envisioned that *Follow Me* will be utilized primarily by:
- Local church groups
- College students
- Volunteer mission teams

An individual can take up this book and gain real benefit from its study and application, but to optimize the experience it is vital that the study be done in community. If God has stirred your interest in prayerwalking and you don't have anyone else to join with you in this endeavor, see yourself as God's chosen vessel to draw together those that He has already been working in and preparing to become prayerwalkers. Small groups of four to twelve are optimal. Perhaps your care group or Sunday school class is ready to be challenged to become in-the-world pray-ers. Offer the experience as part of your church's discipleship curriculum. Utilize it in small-group Bible studies that are already part of your campus ministry or use it as part of the foundational training of a mission team. Gather those who are already people of prayer and go through the study together. Women's mission and/or ministry groups as well as Promise Keepers-type groups are logical choices. Ask your elders or deacons to deepen their walk with Christ and expand the effectiveness of their ministry by journeying through the study together. God is calling His people out into the world as on-site intercessors. He will use you to accomplish this. Make yourself available to Him to this end and ask Him to show you the group you are to facilitate.

Structure

If you have not already read the introduction to the book, please turn to page 1 and do that now before proceeding.

Now that you've read the introduction, you have a basic understanding of what prayerwalking is and how this *Follow Me* study is intended to be used.

First Meeting

The first meeting of your group can be at any time during the week before your study together actually begins, although near the end of the week or during the weekend would be best. It only needs to be for an hour. A suggested outline for this first meeting follows:

1. Begin with a welcome and ensure that everyone knows each other.

2. Then lead the group in prayer, exalting God and committing yourselves to be His servants. Ask Him specifically to bond you together as a group during this study and transform each of you into prayerwalkers.

3. Hand out copies of the book.

4. Using the introduction as a resource, share the basics of what prayerwalking is and its history.

5. Then from the "About This Study" section, begin to explain the individual and group aspects of the study. Have the participants turn to the first day's study and follow along as you explain. Answer any questions that may arise.

6. When everyone understands their daily, personal responsibilities, explain the weekend group meetings. Two hours will be required for each weekend meeting. Ideally a time should be found that can remain constant throughout the study. (Remember a prayerwalk will be part of your group gathering each week beginning with week 2, so consider the need for daylight as you choose a meeting time. Also, you may meet at the campus ministry center or the church to begin with, but by week 3 you could be meeting in different places to coincide with nearby prayerwalk locations.)

7. Ask the group to make a mutual commitment to be faithful in completing their daily study each morning of the week and ask them to commit to pray for one another as they establish this discipline. Stress to them that their weekly group meeting will include discussion of their experiences with the biblical material and its daily application in their lives as developing prayer-walkers.

8. Encourage them to commit to memory each week's key Scripture and remind them to also bring their books and Bibles to each weekly meeting.

9. Close with a time of prayer, asking at least two or three of the group to voice prayers. Knowing your group, you may want to ask these in advance to be ready to pray. Close the group prayertime, asking God to help and have His way in each person's life as your begin this journey together.

Note: As facilitator, put as one of your top priorities daily prayer, by name, for each member of the group as they work through the first week. Particularly ask God to convict and show any member who does not know Christ as personal Savior their true condition and God's ready provision. Pray for their salvation.

Week 1: Walking with God

Gather and Pray

Once everyone is present, quiet the group and begin with a time of giving God thanks for the ways that He personally demonstrated His love and grace in their lives during the past week. Gently encourage everyone to pray if they will. Exalt God with expressions of praise as you worship together.

Review and Respond

Ask the group what this week's key Scripture was. If you have a marker board, write it on the board as they recite it.

Discuss the three key parts of the Scripture. Note what we are to love, how we are to relate to others, and what will characterize our life before God. Guide the discussion with questions such as:

• For what did God create us in the beginning? (to walk with Him)
• How was this great privilege lost?
• Is there hope for a return to our original purpose?
• How? Through whom?

Now, transition to the "Special Invitation" contained in week 1 (p. 12). Ask the group their response to this invitation. Give them opportunity to publicly share their confession of Christ. If this is the case, take time to celebrate this and affirm them in their new life in Christ. Join in a time of grateful prayer. Now ask:

• As new creations in Christ, how are we to live out our daily lives?
• Are we to "act" like Jesus or "be" like Jesus?
• How can we "be"?
• What were the three aiding elements that we discovered? (the word, faith, prayer)
• Who has Jesus sent to enable the ongoing transformation in us?

Transition now to a time of review of the Throughout Today experiences. Each day after we completed our morning study, we had an assignment entitled Throughout Today.

• How did you do in these?
• Was it difficult? Hard to stay focused? Why?
• What was easiest? Why?

Now turn to day 4 and discuss C. S. Lewis' words.

- How are we to respond to the Spirit's transforming work in us?
- Did you find yourself resisting or disliking some of the work the Spirit has attempted in you? What? How?

Now turn to day 5 and talk about Jesus' words in John 15:1–5.

- How does He portray Himself? Us?
- What is the one essential to ensure that His life fills and flows in us?

Now let's look at day 5's Throughout Today questions.

- Discuss any points of resistance that surfaced during the week.
- Talk about why we resist the Spirit's work in us.

Lastly, let's reflect upon this week's Evening Reflections.

- Were you able to discipline yourself to do this?
- Why was it hard? Easy?
- What are the benefits?

Stress that in subsequent weeks we will not be spending as much time reviewing the past week's study. Affirm the importance of being diligent in completing all aspects of the daily study and disciplining ourselves throughout each day in light of guiding thoughts and suggestions.

Closing

Be sensitive to direct the closing prayertime in line with what the members personally experienced through the study. Celebration may be in order. Some may need support and encouragement. Personal needs may illumine the opportunity to minister through prayer to others.

Close the time with expressions of gratitude to God for His redeeming love and expressed commitment to follow Him forward, allowing Him to work in each one as He desires.

Before dismissing, remind the participants that next week they will be participating in their first group prayerwalk. In preparation, ask them to review the basic prayerwalkers preparation outline found on page 97. Exhort them to be careful in their responsiveness to the Holy Spirit as He prepares them to be useable vessels on this prayerwalk. Also, remind them to dress accordingly with comfortable walking shoes.

Ensure that next week's meeting is held in a location where the group can walk out of the building and into an area where they can prayerwalk. This is important to save the time that would be needed to drive to another location.

Week 2: Following Jesus as Prayerwalkers

Gather and Pray

Quieting the group, lead them into a time of prayer, thanking Him for His gracious work in and teaching of them this past week. Encourage them to pray out of this past week's experiences and then invite God to guide them as they step out on their first prayerwalk.

Review and Respond

Highlight this week's key Scripture. Point out the truth that when we follow Christ, we never walk in darkness but rather have light and life.

Give each person an opportunity to share an important truth that God taught them during the past week. Then ask them to share a point at which they are struggling in their walk with Christ. Help each other as appropriate and stop and pray if the situation calls for it.

Now ask them the three types of prayerwalking. Which is essential to the effectiveness of the other two? Why?

Prayerwalk

Now it is time for the group to go out on its first intentional prayerwalk together. Ask them to turn to page 97 in their book. Review with them the basic steps in "Stepping Out."

Ask the group to form into pairs. Married individuals should go with their spouse or someone of the same sex. Plan forty-five minutes for the prayerwalk. Ask the groups to spread out and go in various directions. Encourage them to move slowly, pausing as necessary. Remind them to be attentive to the Holy Spirit's guidance and pray in light of it. Give them a time to be back at the meeting place. As soon as each team gets out into the neighborhood, ask them to begin by praying aloud, "Lord, guide us, use us, teach us." He will.

Now have everyone stand and, without telling them to bow their heads and close their eyes, begin to pray for the teams, keeping your eyes open and your head up. This will begin to sensitize the prayerwalkers to this new attitude of prayer.

Depending upon the outside temperature, have hot or cold drinks ready when they return. After regathering, allow each member of the group to share what they experienced on their first prayerwalk.

- Encourage interaction.
- Note what the Spirit revealed or spoke.
- How did they respond?
- Did anyone miss His guidance?
- What aspects of these first two weeks of study were particularly important?
- Did God give a particular Scripture that guided or illumined your prayer?

Closing

As you prepare to complete this session, exhort everyone to continue the disciplines of the first days of study. Tell them that you are praying for them as they wrestle with any sins that are hindering their walk. If appropriate, share a point at which you are struggling or have struggled and ask their prayer for you. Close in prayer, leading them to thank God for each other and for His bringing of them together for this experience. Intercede personally for any member experiencing challenges. Praise God with thanksgiving and ask Him to continue His work and teaching in each member's life.

Remind them of next week's meeting location.

Note: It is important for you to plan ahead for the weekly group prayerwalks. There are several ways for you to do this.

Think strategically. Where has God already been leading your group or church? It could be an area for a new church, a campus outreach such as a new dorm Bible study or an international dinner, a new mission possibility. Plan to take the group there for your meeting and then prayerwalk that area.

Meet in the homes of different members. That way you will prayerwalk a different neighborhood every week.

Book the community room of a local library or a conference room at a police station. Meet there and then go out.

Look within your group and see what avenues God has already given for strategic access to different areas of society. A member may work in government or in a hospital and be able to schedule a meeting room there. Prayerwalk the halls and floors of the building.

Call the pastor of a church whose congregation is made up of a different racial or ethnic background than yours and ask to meet one week in their church. Ask where in the neighborhood you should intercede and how.

If weather permits, consider meeting outside one week in an area where you can look across the city and pray.

There are far more venues for prayerwalking than you will have time to explore. Be open and creative and ask God to show you where He uniquely wants your group to intercede.

Week 3: Praying His Will into the World

Gather and Pray

Listening to the pre-conversation, see if you might find your opening orienting word in something that one of the members is sharing from the study. Quiet the group and as you bow, invite everyone to express their prayers out of the newness of their walk with God. Close this time of prayer with thanksgiving to God for His loving work in you and invite Him to continue that through your discussion and prayerwalk.

Review and Respond

Review the key Scripture. Begin to stimulate discussion of central truths from this week's study and their personal impact and implications.

• What was it like this week as we consciously began to listen to God and respond?

• Any difficulties?

• When you recognized that God was speaking, what did you do? Respond? Resist? (If there was resistance, allow time for discussion at this point)

• What was the testimony against the children of Israel? (Psalm 106:13)

• Was it difficult to wait on God? Why?

• Did Christ show you any areas where your life is at cross purposes with His life in you?

• What should we do about that?

Discuss now the new experience this week of beginning to go on short, daily, personal prayerwalks. Ask the group to share their experiences.

Transition to discussion of some of God's promises and the privileged activity of blessing.

• What does a promise mean to you?

• What does it feel like and what do you think of people when they keep a promise that they made to you?

• What promises did God illumine to you this week as you prayed and prayerwalked?

• Give an example of how you prayed in light of some of these promises.

• On our last day of this week we studied blessing. What was your response to this?

• What is blessing?
• What is the important prerequisite to receptivity to our blessing?
• Review the blessing of Numbers 6:24–26 in preparation to go out on your group prayerwalk.

Prayerwalk

Outline the prayerwalk that is planned and give instructions as necessary. If you are in a new area, directions will be in order.

Review the basics from last week's "Stepping Out" instructions and answer questions/clarify understandings.

Allow people to go with a different partner or team if they would like. There are benefits both in staying with the same partner and praying with another. Give opportunity for both as people would like. Two has been found to be a very effective number for a prayerwalk team. Sidewalks usually aren't wide enough for more than two. Two people can walk together and hear each other easily as they talk and pray. And whether in an American neighborhood or in an overseas nation, two attract less attention than more. If your group does not have an even number of individuals, teams of three are still alright.

If there are questions about why married individuals should prayerwalk with a person of the same sex or their spouse, remind people that prayer is one of the most intimate of human activities and the careful guarding of the sanctity of marriage can be breached by the extended prayer experiences that prayerwalking provides.

Ask the group to be especially alert to pray God's promises as they go and speak His blessings upon the people.

Plan forty-five minutes for the prayerwalk and give the group a time to be back in the room. Have appropriate refreshments ready if possible.

Now, again stand and ask one of the group to lead in prayer as you head out. Remind everyone to pray with their heads up and their eyes open.

Once the group is regathered, quiet them and begin a time of sharing out of the prayerwalking experience. A new element that we want to introduce at this point is that of beginning to listen to what God is saying to and through the prayerwalkers. He will be revealing His heart and His will and where He is at work in that neighborhood. The group needs to recognize this and be attentive when God is speaking something specific through the body. Note these whenever they occur and either act upon them as a group or share them with the campus ministry leader or pastor. In some cases God may direct a *Follow Me* group to prayerwalk in the same area every week in anticipation of His doing a new work there. Obey.

During this post-prayerwalk time help the group to understand how God is using them to extend His kingdom into an area.

Encourage them to help one another as they experience new depths of God's love and desire for people.

Ask them to share what they are experiencing as they prayerwalk both personally and corporately.

Closing

In your departing prayer, pray particularly for God's help for the group to stay disciplined in their daily study and activities. Close by blessing the group with elements from the blessing in 1 Kings 8:56–61.

Note: Next week is a critical week as God shapes your group into men and women who will wholeheartedly follow Christ. Day 3 will be a particularly critical day.

Be faithful to intercede every day this week for everyone that God may prepare them to respond in obedience regardless of the pain or cost.

Week 4: Prayerwalking and Ministry in Community

Gather and Pray

Read this week's key Scripture as you prepare the group to settle in and bow before God. Then ask two or three of the group to voice the group's thoughts and desires with words of thanksgiving for Jesus who is the Light of the world, for His life in us, and for the way people saw Him and His gracious work in the group members this past week.

Review and Respond

Begin by inquiring how the discipline of Evening Reflection is going. Some of the group may be lagging a bit by now. Reinforce the importance of getting still before God to look back upon the day and see Him in it. Remind them how good thanks and gratitude are to Him. Ensure that those who are doing well get to share at this point as an encouragement to the others.

Now begin the discussion time with the orientation focus of our worship and service—i.e. God, not man. Ask the group to share what they learned about worship this week. What happens when we worship? (Psalm 22:3) Move to a discussion of perspective. Ask:

• What does it mean to "keep looking down?"

• What is a situation that you have been viewing from the world's perspective but this week began to see from heaven's perspective?

Carefully move the discussion to the day 3 focus. Say: Remember the single mom in the church who went out on a prayerwalk with another lady, only to discover that the area where God had sent them was the very area where her husband lived with his mistress. Ask: This week did God show you a barrier in your life that you have been unwilling for Him to remove?

Allow there to be silence here. Do not move beyond this point quickly. God has likely been working in many lives and this is the time when decisions to forgive and turn loose can be made and affirmed. Ensure that this is a time when that can happen. Minister to and pray for one another as needed.

Quite likely you will want to have a time of prayerful thanksgiving and praise of God for His liberating love. Do that.

Reminding them of the unique opportunity of the garbage truck driver, explore with the group the special opportunities that God has given them to pray on-site in their community. Ensure that everyone understands at least one way they can be unique incidental prayerwalkers. Help one another to this insight.

Prayerwalk

In preparation for this weekend's prayerwalk, ask individuals if they had an encounter this week in one of their personal prayerwalks where they had opportunity to ask someone personally if they could pray for them. Have them share these experiences.

Now give instructions and information as needed to go out on this week's prayerwalk. The same time and parameters will apply this week and each week. Ask if there are any questions and, if not, have the group stand (they should be used to heads-up, open-eyed praying by now) and ask someone to send them out with a prayer of promise and faith.

Have the refreshments ready when they return and get the group settled as quickly as possible.

Begin to debrief this prayerwalk. Remind them to be listening for God's voice in the testimonies. As the group talks about their experience, be alert to inject truths that were already learned in past week's studies. Affirm these wherever you can. Be careful to keep the session within the agreed-upon two-hour time frame.

Closing

Close this week's gathering by turning to Luke 9 and reading aloud verses 57–62. Make your last words a repeat of those in verse 57, "I will follow You wherever You go."

Pray for the group, confessing their desire to truly and completely follow Christ and ask His help at any point of struggle.

Week 5: Prayerwalking and Enemy Opposition

Gather and Pray

Again begin by reading this week's key Scripture. Ask the group to unite their hearts and voices in praising God for His victory over the enemy through Jesus and exalt Christ for His faithfulness, even unto death, for us that we might be set free from sin and death and the devil. Invite Him to have His way in the group today and through the group as they go out to pray.

Review and Respond

Ask each one to share what became most real to them this week as they studied the topic of spiritual warfare. After they have shared, ask:
• How did we learn that the New Testament church responded to attacks?
• How did they pray?
• How did they then continue to live?

Reiterate the importance of not being drawn into dialogue or dispute with the enemy. Deprive him of this pleasure and stay focused on Christ and unbroken communion with Him.
• What were the four central elements of the New Testament church's spiritual warfare strategy?
• Which of these were you most surprised to discover?
• Have you incorporated each of the four into your life?
• Which ones were missing?

Now move to the personal experience of the members.
• Has anyone experienced any spiritual warfare this week?
• Share it with us.
• Did we respond correctly?

Now recap the three primary forces that hinder us in following Christ.
• What are they?
• Which pieces of the armor particularly relate to each of these?

Prayerwalk

Remind the group that all intercession is spiritual warfare and that prayerwalking is invasionary intercession. Strengthen them with this reminder so that they are already alert to this reality and ready with all pieces of the armor in place.

Give specific instructions and information related to today's prayerwalk. If there is any fear or anxiety, counter these with prayer. Before the team prays and goes out, ask them to turn to Psalm 31:14. Lead them through the three confessions/declarations: "You are my God," "I trust in You," "My times are in Your hands."

Stand and pray, commending the team into God's strong hands, rejoicing in Christ's ever-present victory and praying God's kingdom come, God's will be done in their lives and in the area where they are going to prayerwalk.

When the teams have returned and gotten something to drink, sit down and begin to talk about the prayerwalk and this week's focus. Ensure that Jesus is the focus and that the enemy does not receive any attention. Strengthen people's faith with Scripture and testimony. Prepare to close by reading again verses 18–20 of Ephesians 6. Reiterate unceasing prayer and communion with Christ, ever-alertness, and bold gracious speaking of the truth into situations and sensitized lives.

Note any specific directions that God may have given and remember to share this with leaders. Make adjustments in future prayerwalk plans as God may have led.

Closing

Affirm the group for their faithfulness as they enter this last week of *Follow Me*. Rejoice together over what God has done in and through them and how He has worked in lives. Thank Him for the new liberty that He has brought and the precious bonding that exists in the group. Pray for one another and commit to finish this study with renewed diligence and faith. Specifically ask Him to give the grace of conviction at any point where resistance to Christ's lordship is still present. Exalt the Lord together.

Week 6: Prayerwalking that All the World May Know

Gather and Pray

As your group begins this last session together, think back over what you've experienced together. Briefly share highlights and then let these be the starters for your time of group praise and prayer.

Review and Respond

This last time of sharing and reflecting is very important to help the group recognize where God may be directing toward future specific prayerwalking activities and initiatives. Be sensitive to give enough time for each of the below sections and note, for later sharing with the appropriate person(s), what the group understands God has said and shown. Begin by asking:

• Do prayer and prayerwalking have the vital place in our church or campus ministry that they should have?

• If not, why not?

    In our church/campus ministry:

• Has God said or shown anything specific that we need to carefully consider for adjustment/inclusion in our church/group?

• What?

    In our local community:

• What has He shown us He wants to do with and through on-site prayer right here?

    In our city:

• How might He be leading us to unite with other believers to blanket our city in regular faithful on-site intercession?

    In our world:

• What has He said to us regarding the world?

• Where might He be leading our church/campus ministry to go, and where may He be leading us as prayerwalkers to go and prepare the way of the Lord?

Prayerwalk

As you now prepare to go out on your last prayerwalk as a *Follow Me* group, ask the group to share a highlight or two from one of the earlier prayerwalks.

Rejoice together over what God did and remind the group that He wants to continue doing this kind of work in and through each of them as they are faithful to be Spirit-filled on-site pray-ers.

Give instructions for today's prayerwalk and then stand for your committal prayer.

When the teams return, gather and debrief once more the experiences of the various teams.

Make this point: It is always important to regather after every intentional prayerwalk and share what God did and said. One reason is that it enables the Body of Christ to give Him praise and thanks. It also is very powerful in encouraging believers that God is active and present in their world and that He wants to speak to and use them. Lastly, the church needs to learn to hear God through one another as He speaks to and through the body. Listening to each other pray and hearing testimony of how God revealed are vital to healthy life as a church.

Closing

As you prepare to close this last session, share two important, anchoring words with the group.

Read Isaiah 30:21, "This is the way, walk in it." Yes!

As we continue to follow Christ in an unwavering walk of prayer and faith, remember a responsibility which is now ours. 2 Timothy 2:2: "And the things which you have heard from me in the presence of many witnesses, these entrust to faithful men, who will be able to teach others also."

Be faithful to take other believers out prayerwalking with you and teach them the basics of what God has taught you in these weeks. Be ready and willing to facilitate another *Follow Me* group as God continues to turn His church into a praying and a prayerwalking church.

Close by joining hands and committing yourselves to follow Him wherever He leads and to pray until His kingdom has come in all the earth.

Amen and God bless you.

Available from New Hope Publishers
    (at 1-800-968-7301 or www.wmustore.com)
Follow Me: Becoming a Lifestyle Prayerwalker by Randy Sprinkle
    (New Hope, 2005).

Available from the International Mission Board
    (at 1-800-866-3621 or www.imb.org/resources)
Prayerwalking: Praying On-Site with Insight by Steve Hawthorne and
    Graham Kendrick (Creation House, 1993).
Prayer Journeys: A Leader's How-to Manual (Caleb Project, 1995). An
    excellent resource to prepare a prayerwalking team for overseas service.

Available from the North American Mission Board
    (at 1-800-448-8032 or www.namb.net/root/resources)
Taking Prayer to the Streets—A comprehensive resource for local churches
    who desire to implement a complete in-the-community prayer ministry.
Prayer Journeys Pocket Guide (available in English and Spanish)
Lighthouses of Prayer Starter Kit—Information for starting a neighborhood
    prayer ministry.

Available from Waymakers
    (by calling 1-800-264-5214 or at www.waymakers.org)
Prayerwalking: Praying On-Site with Insight by Steve Hawthorne and
    Graham Kendrick (Creation House, 1993).
Prayerwalk Organizer Guide by Steve Hawthorne. An excellent resource to
    help you organize and conduct a city-wide prayerwalk.
Prayerwalk Team Kit by Steve Hawthorne. Basic equipping kit for
    prayerwalk teams.
Prompts for Prayerwalkers by Steve Hawthorne.

Resources

Published by Arcadia Publishing,
an imprint of Tempus Publishing, Inc.
3047 N. Lincoln Ave., Suite 410
Chicago, IL 60657

Printed in Great Britain.

Library of Congress Catalog Card Number: 2001092767

For all general information contact Arcadia Publishing at:
Telephone 843-853-2070
Fax 843-853-0044
E-Mail sales@arcadiapublishing.com

For customer service and orders:
Toll-Free 1-888-313-2665

Visit us on the internet at http://www.arcadiapublishing.com

A typical South Shore street, Oglesby Avenue runs the length of the neighborhood.

IMAGES
of America

CHICAGO'S
SOUTH SHORE

Charles Celander

ARCADIA

The author's father, Hugo (Hugh) W. Celander Jr., and grandfather, Hugo W. Celander Sr., stroll through South Shore in November 1924. Hugh Celander Jr. became a local photographer whose own photographs, along with other collected images, are featured in this book. Hugo Celander Sr. was in real estate. This book, which chronicles the development of Chicago's South Shore area through the use of historic photographs, is dedicated to them.